Recipes Worth Sharing

by Janet Majure

BREAD BASKET PUBLISHING COMPANY

Recipes Worth Sharing
By Janet Majure

ISBN 0-9656695-0-5

10 9 8 7 6 5 4 3 2 1

Breadbasket Publishing Company
P.O. Box 1161
Lawrence, KS 66044-0161

Printed in the United States of America

*In loving memory
of my mother,
who first taught
me to cook.*

Contents

Acknowledgments

Special thanks go to the hundreds of cooks featured in "Come Into My Kitchen," the weekly column about home cooks in *The Kansas City Star*. They have willingly and enthusiastically shared their favorite recipes with other people who love to cook, and their contributions are the basis of this collection.

Thanks to Jill Silva, my supportive editor at the *Star*; the *Star* copy desk; John Martellaro, who hired me for "Come Into My Kitchen"; and the uncounted readers who have suggested cooks for the column.

Lyn Foister copyedited this book, Traci Bunkers designed it, and Myia Williams proofread it. All three have made this book as smooth-reading and attractive as it is.

I'm grateful to the people, including my late husband John Lee, who have cultivated my cooking and my love of food over the years. Thanks to my daughter, Susan, my father and stepmother, Dave and Jeff Majure, and other family members for their support in this project. Friends, too, have been invaluable and, happily for me, too numerous to name. Still, I must mention Susan Fitzgerald, Judith Galas, Sue Newton, Mary Lou Nolan and Lynn Byczynski.

Introduction

People who love to cook often cite the pleasure of sharing good food as the main reason they enjoy cooking. Cooking for others is a gift of love and friendship, appreciated as much by the giver as by the recipient.

Equally valued by the cook is the satisfaction of sharing favorite recipes with others. (Although they exist, cooks who keep their recipes from others are rare.) More than 200 such cooks, for no compensation, have shared their recipes with me, and they've shared some wonderful ones. These women and men have allowed me into their homes to talk about their cooking and to take their pictures to appear in "Come Into My Kitchen," the long-running column in *The Kansas City Star*.

As a group, they are a humble lot. As often as not, these cooks are quick to say that a recipe isn't really theirs. They point out that their recipes are based on ones they got from their mother, a friend, a relative or a favorite cookbook or magazine. Yet, each cook brings to a recipe his or her own interpretation.

Similarly, this recipe collection bears the marks of its collector. I tend to favor fresh foods, easily and quickly prepared but full of flavor, and that notion is reflected in my selections. Still, while most of the recipes are healthful, many are not. I think there is a place for both.

I have greatly enjoyed meeting and talking with cooks in the five years I've been writing "Come Into My Kitchen." Food is a marvelous means of bringing people together. Thanks to "Come Into My Kitchen," I've met women and men of all ages from far-reaching backgrounds, all eager to share their stories through food. I thank them for the opportunity to do so.

In my kitchen, the best recipes bear the greatest number of stains. Cookbook pages are warped from handling, recipe cards are dotted with spills and drips. *Recipes Worth Sharing* is a collection of just such recipes, favored by their contributors with the marks of much use and appreciation. My hope is that readers will make *Recipes Worth Sharing* their own well-stained cookbook.

I invite readers to send questions or comments to me at P.O. Box 1161, Lawrence, KS 66044-0161.

Janet Majure

For Starters

Hors d'Oeuvres & Snacks, Appetizers & First Courses

Empanadas de Queso (Cheese Turnovers)

Maggie Rotenberg, Leawood, Kansas

For dough:
2 (3 oz) packages cream cheese
½ cup (1 stick) butter
2 cups all-purpose flour
1 tsp salt
7 to 8 tsp water
1 egg beaten until smooth with ¼ tsp
   salt

For filling:
2 tbsp butter
¼ cup finely chopped onion
2 tsp all-purpose flour
¼ tsp salt
¾ cup milk
1½ cups (6 oz) shredded Monterey
   Jack or mozzarella cheese

Maggie draws on her South American and European roots in many of her recipes.

1. Make dough: Place cream cheese and butter in medium bowl. Mash with fork until smooth. Push to one side of bowl; add flour and salt to other side. Use fork to lift cheese mixture on top of flour.

With a pastry blender or fork, cut cheese mixture into flour until pieces are the size of small peas.

Add 7 teaspoons water and toss with fork until all flour is moistened and mixture starts to form a ball. If necessary, add remaining 1 teaspoon water to crumbs in bottom of bowl.

Shape mixture into a ball and flatten. Preheat oven to 400 degrees.

2. Make filling: Melt butter in small saucepan over medium heat. Add onion and sauté, stirring occasionally until tender, about 10 minutes; do not brown.

Stir in flour and salt until blended.

Add milk. Stir constantly until mixture comes to a full boil. Stir and boil 1 minute. Stir in cheese; set aside.

3. Cut dough into 2 equal portions. On a lightly floured surface, roll out 1 portion to ⅛-inch thickness. Using a plastic lid or large biscuit cutter, cut dough into 3-inch circles.

4. Lightly knead scraps and let rest 3 to 5 minutes. Roll and cut circles and repeat process until all of 1 dough portion is used. As you work, you may stack circles on flat surface.

5. For each circle, lightly brush beaten egg-salt mixture around edge to make ¼-inch border. Place 1 rounded teaspoon of filling on circle, keeping filling off egg-coated border. Fold circle in half over filling, bringing edges together. Press edges together with a fork.

6. Use knife point to make 1 or 2 small slits in top of each empanada. Lightly brush tops with egg mixture. Place about ¼ inch apart on ungreased baking sheets. Repeat with remaining dough and filling. If desired, refrigerate a day or two, until 15 minutes before serving.

7. Bake 10 to 12 minutes, until golden brown. Also may be baked in advance and rewarmed.

Makes 30 to 35 appetizers

Olive- and Cheese-Stuffed Braided Bread

Jennifer Furla, Kansas City, Missouri

1 package (3 loaves) frozen white bread dough
1 (8 oz) jar pimento-stuffed green cocktail olives
1 (15.5 oz) can pitted ripe black olives
2 tbsp olive oil
8 ounces coarsely grated Gruyere, mozzarella, Swiss or a white-cheese blend

Jennifer had tasted a bread similar to this one and developed her own recipe when she needed something to take to a party. Since she's not a baker, she used frozen bread dough.

1. Thaw bread dough and allow to rise according to package directions. (Be sure to check package in advance to allow enough preparation time.)

2. While the bread is rising, drain liquid from the green and black olives and process in food processor until finely chopped. Set aside.

3. Preheat oven to 350 degrees. Lightly grease a large baking sheet with vegetable shortening or nonstick cooking spray.

4. Gently roll each dough ball between your hands to form three long ropes, about 24 inches each. Lay the ropes on the baking sheet parallel to one another, and press ropes together at one end. Brush lightly with olive oil.

5. Position baking sheet so joined ends are away from you. Begin a braid: Gently lay right-hand rope over center rope, then lay left-hand rope over the new center rope. Spread a small amount of olive mixture and grated cheese on center rope at junction with other dough ropes. Cover most of the cheese and olive mixture as you repeat braiding process. Add part of the olive mixture and cheese at center after each round of braiding. Continue until entire loaf is braided, and all of olive mixture and cheese is used.

6. Bake 45 minutes, or until bread is lightly browned and no longer doughy in the center. It should separate easily into segments when pulled with a fork. Cool on baking sheet. Serve warm, either by cutting in slices or by pulling off each braided section. Goes well with hearty soup or light pasta, or as an appetizer or for brunch or cocktail buffet. Freezes well.

Makes 1 large loaf

"Devil" Eggs

Diane Conner, Leawood, Kansas

"We're into tailgate parties for baseball and football," Diane says, "so I do things that are easily portable or feed a lot of people."

1. Put eggs in medium saucepan and cover with cold water. Bring to a boil. Remove from heat and let stand, covered, 10 minutes. Drain. Peel shells from eggs while holding them under cold running water.

2. Cut eggs in half lengthwise. Remove yolks and mix with mayonnaise, horseradish, vinegar, mustard, dill relish, salt, pepper and sugar. Use mixture to fill egg white.

3. Garnish with a dab of your favorite salsa and top with a slice of jalapeno.

Note: These are hot! The faint-hearted might want to start with 1 teaspoon horseradish, then add more to taste.

Makes 6 servings

6 eggs
2 tbsp mayonnaise
1 tbsp prepared horseradish
1 tbsp vinegar
1 tsp mustard
1 tsp dill relish
½ tsp salt
½ tsp pepper
1 tsp sugar
Salsa, optional
Sliced canned jalapeno peppers

Crab-Stuffed Mushrooms

Elaine Carlson, Overland Park, Kansas

12 large mushroom caps
½ cup (1 stick) butter or margarine
1 (6 oz) can crabmeat, drained
¼ cup fresh lemon juice, or to taste
1 tbsp minced garlic, or to taste
¼ cup white wine
Monterey Jack cheese slices, cut into
    12 (1-inch) squares
Lemon wedges
Parsley sprigs

1. Clean mushrooms with a fine brush; pull out and reserve stems. Place mushrooms, empty side up, close together in a baking dish or pie plate.

2. Mince mushroom stems. Melt butter or margarine in a medium skillet. Add minced mushroom stems, and sauté until tender. Add the crabmeat, lemon juice, garlic and white wine. Cook over low heat about 10 minutes until the liquid has evaporated. Adjust seasonings to taste.

3. Fill mushroom caps with the crabmeat mixture, and top each with a square of Monterey Jack cheese.

4. Bake at 350 degrees about 20 minutes, or until cheese has melted. Serve with fresh lemon wedges and parsley on small plates with cocktail fork, or keep on warming plate for buffet with lemon wedges on the side.

Makes 12 hors d'oeuvres or 6 first-course servings

Low-Fat Party Mix

Shirley Grout, Kansas City, Missouri

Shirley's home economics students at Eastgate Middle School make this recipe.

1. In large baking pan, combine Corn Chex, Rice Chex, Crispix, shredded wheat, toasted oat cereal, pretzels and popcorn. As you add each ingredient to the pan, spray very lightly with nonstick cooking spray. This will help mixture absorb the seasonings. Stir.

2. Combine Worcestershire sauce, Tabasco and liquid smoke. Sprinkle over cereal mixture, and stir several times.

3. Combine cayenne pepper, hickory-smoked salt, salt substitute, garlic powder and butter powder. Sprinkle over the party mix, stirring several times.

4. Bake at 250 degrees 1 hour, stirring every 20 minutes.

Makes 2½ quarts

1 cup Corn Chex cereal
1 cup Rice Chex cereal
1 cup Crispix cereal
1 cup bite-size shredded wheat
1 cup toasted oat O's cereal
2 cups fat-free stick pretzels
3 cups air-popped popcorn
Nonstick cooking spray
1 tbsp Worcestershire sauce
½ tsp Tabasco sauce
½ tsp liquid smoke
⅛ tsp cayenne pepper
¼ tsp hickory-smoked salt
½ tsp salt substitute, such as
    Mrs. Dash
¼ tsp garlic powder
1 tbsp imitation butter powder, such
    as Molly McButter

Mexican Dip

Betty Charpentier, Lenexa, Kansas

3 medium ripe avocados
2 tbsp lemon juice
½ tsp salt
¼ tsp ground black pepper
8 ounces sour cream
½ cup mayonnaise or mayonnaise-
  style salad dressing
1 (1⅛ oz) envelope taco seasoning
  mix
2 (10.5 oz) cans plain or jalapeno
  bean dip
1 large bunch green onions,
  including tender green tops,
  chopped (about 1 cup chopped)
3 medium tomatoes, chopped (about
  2 cups chopped)
2 (2.25 oz) cans sliced ripe olives,
  drained
1 (8 oz) package shredded sharp
  cheddar cheese
Tortilla chips

This dip is a standard at the Charpentier family's annual Super Bowl party.

1. Peel, pit and mash avocados in bowl with lemon juice, salt and pepper.

2. Combine sour cream, mayonnaise and taco seasoning in separate bowl.

3. Line bottom and sides of 7½- by 11½-inch glass baking dish with bean dip. Cover bottom and sides with avocado mixture. Cover with sour cream mixture. Sprinkle with green onions, tomatoes and olives. Cover with shredded cheese.

4. Cover and refrigerate until ready to serve. Serve with tortilla chips.

Makes 12 servings

Jo's Hot Sauce

Joan Lombardino, Kansas City, Missouri

1. Place all ingredients in large pan over medium heat; bring to boil, stirring so that mixture doesn't stick or burn. Reduce heat and simmer 1 hour, stirring occasionally.

2. Have hot, clean jars and lids ready for canning. Fill jars, cap and process 15 minutes in boiling bath to seal. If you prefer, serve fresh.

Notes: For quicker preparation, chop ingredients in food processor, starting with garlic, then habaneros, jalapenos, onion, bell peppers and tomatoes, but take care to leave mixture somewhat chunky. For hotter mixture, include some jalapeno or habanero seeds. Especially if chopping by hand, wear rubber gloves and wash cutting surface, knives and hands immediately after preparing jalapeno and habanero peppers.

Makes about 8 quarts

8 quarts fresh or canned tomatoes, coarsely chopped
2 cups chopped mixture of red and green bell peppers
2 cups chopped onion
1 cup chopped jalapeno peppers, seeds removed
¼ cup finely chopped habanero peppers, seeds removed
4 cloves garlic, finely chopped
12 ounces tomato paste
⅔ cup wine vinegar
⅔ cup sugar
¼ tsp ground cumin
¼ tsp dried oregano
¼ cup lime juice

Italian Layered Dip

Debbie Hutchison, Leawood, Kansas

½ cup mayonnaise
1 clove garlic, cut in half
1 tsp dried sweet basil
¼ cup lemon juice
1 small dried chili
2 (8 oz) packages cream cheese, softened
1 (12 oz) bottle cocktail sauce
1 (6 oz) can black olives, chopped
1 small red onion, diced
1 (6 oz) can tiny shrimp, drained
4 ounces pepperoni, chopped
1 cup shredded mozzarella cheese
1 cup shredded cheddar cheese
Corn chips or assorted crackers

1. In blender or food processor, blend mayonnaise, garlic, basil, lemon juice and dried chili on high 30 seconds. Add cream cheese and mix to blend.

2. Spread the mixture in a 10- to 12-inch oval dish with 1- to 2-inch sides. Spread cocktail sauce over cream cheese. Add, in layers, olives, red onion, shrimp, pepperoni, mozzarella and cheddar cheese.

3. Cover tightly and refrigerate overnight. Serve with corn chips or assorted crackers.

Makes 12 to 15 servings

White Queso

Debbie Kennedy, Mission Hills, Kansas

1 cup mayonnaise
1½ cups grated Parmesan cheese
1 cup grated Monterey Jack cheese
2 (4 oz) cans chopped green chilies, undrained
¼ tsp cumin
⅛ tsp chili powder
Cayenne pepper, to taste
Tortilla chips

This dip is a variation on a recipe Debbie found in a magazine.

1. Combine mayonnaise, Parmesan, Monterey Jack, chilies and their liquid, cumin, chili powder and cayenne.

2. Put in 3½- to 4-cup casserole, and bake at 350 degrees 20 minutes, or until top begins to brown. Serve hot with tortilla chips.

Makes 3 cups

Hot Crab Dip

Susie Trupp, Overland Park, Kansas

"I've always loved hors d'oeuvres," says Susie. "I love the 'snacky' type things."

1. Blend cream cheese and mayonnaise. Add remaining ingredients, and mix well.

2. Transfer to 1- to 1½-quart baking dish (about 7 inches in diameter or square), and bake at 350 degrees until bubbly, about 15 minutes. Serve with crackers.

Makes about 2 cups

1 (8 oz) package cream cheese, at
　　room temperature
½ cup mayonnaise
1 (6 oz) can white crabmeat, drained
　　and flaked
½ tsp garlic salt
½ tsp curry powder
¼ cup finely chopped onion
2 tsp prepared mustard
Crackers

Three-Onion Spread

Becci West, Kansas City, Missouri

This looks great served in a hollowed-out red or yellow bell pepper.

1. Heat oil in 10-inch skillet over medium heat. Cook sweet onions and red onions in oil 5 minutes, stirring occasionally, until tender. Stir in parsley and cream cheese until smooth.

2. Spoon into small bowl. Serve warm or cold with crackers. Refrigerate any remaining spread.

Makes 1½ cups

2 tbsp olive or vegetable oil
1 cup chopped sweet onion, such as
　　Vidalia
1 cup chopped red onion
1 tbsp chopped fresh parsley
1 (8 oz) container soft cream cheese
　　with chives and onion
Assorted crackers

Chicken Nut Pâté

Beth Legler, Blue Springs, Missouri

1 cup pecan halves
1 cup walnut halves
2 tbsp crystallized ginger
2 cloves garlic
1 pound boneless, skinless chicken
    breast halves, cooked and cubed
1 cup mayonnaise
2 tbsp soy sauce
1 tbsp Worcestershire sauce
2 tsp white wine vinegar
½ cup minced green onions
Crackers or bread sticks

The recipe is adapted from *The Bess Collection*, which Beth helped produce.

1. In a food processor bowl with chopping blade, combine pecans and walnuts. Process until nuts are coarsely ground. Scrape out of processor bowl.

2. Place ginger and garlic in processor; process until ginger sticks to sides of bowl. Add chicken; process until fine. Add mayonnaise, soy sauce, Worcestershire and vinegar; cycle processor on and off until well-processed. Remove this pâté to a mixing bowl, and fold in green onions and ground nuts.

3. Spoon mixture into 3- to 4-cup serving dish and cover. Chill thoroughly, preferably overnight. Serve with crackers or bread sticks. If you prefer, line a mold with plastic wrap, letting excess wrap drape over sides. Fill with pâté and chill thoroughly. When ready to serve, pull plastic wrap at edges to remove pâté from mold. Pâté keeps well and freezes well.

Note: If desired, reserve a few nuts to garnish unmolded pâté.

Makes 10 servings

Mushroom Pâté

Darlene Walker, Overland Park, Kansas

1. Sauté chopped onions in oil over medium heat until transparent. Add mushrooms, garlic and sherry. Sauté 2 minutes until mushrooms begin to give liquid. Stir in rosemary, thyme, tamari, salt and basil.

2. Put green onions, celery, walnuts and bread crumbs in food processor and process until minced. Add to mushroom mixture, and serve as spread with cracker bread or crackers.

Note: This may be refrigerated. Allow to sit about 15 minutes at room temperature before serving.

Makes 4 to 6 first-course servings

1 tablespoon vegetable oil
1 small onion, chopped
1 1/2 cups chopped mushrooms
3 cloves garlic, minced
2 tbsp cooking sherry
1 tsp dried rosemary
1/2 tsp dried thyme
1 tbsp tamari
1/2 tsp salt
1/2 tsp basil
2 green onions, chopped
2 stalks celery
1/3 cup chopped walnuts
1/2 cup bread crumbs
Cracker bread or crackers

Tapenade Served in Artichokes

Pat and Larry Lillis, Kansas City, Missouri

½ cup kalamata olives
¼ cup Sicilian olives
2 anchovy fillets packed in oil,
    drained and patted dry
4 cloves garlic, peeled, divided
1 tbsp tuna, drained
1 tbsp lemon juice
1 cup fresh basil leaves
¼ cup extra-virgin olive oil
¼ cup mayonnaise, optional
2 large or 3 medium artichokes
4 lemon slices

The recipe doubles easily. For a variation, try making tapenade without the basil.

1. To make tapenade, combine kalamata olives, Sicilian olives, anchovies, 2 cloves garlic, tuna, lemon juice and basil leaves in a food processor fitted with steel blade; process until smooth. While processor is running, slowly drizzle oil into mixture. If desired, blend with mayonnaise to make a lighter sauce. Mixture may be refrigerated up to a week.

2. Lay each artichoke on its side and, using sharp knife, cut off top ¼ inch to ½ inch of artichoke, removing tips of most leaves. Place water in a saucepan for steaming; lightly salt water and add 2 remaining cloves peeled garlic and lemon slices to water. Place artichokes in steamer basket over the water. Steam about 40 minutes, or until a leaf easily pulls away from the stem. Drain artichokes upside down.

3. When cool enough to handle, grasp center bunch of leaves with fingertips and pull gently to remove and form a hollow inside the artichoke. Fill cavity with tapenade. Serve as a first course surrounded by cooked, peeled shrimp, or serve tapenade with French bread as an hors d'oeuvre.

Makes 2 to 3 servings

Devilish Deviled Crab Appetizer

Mildred Hayward, Kansas City, Missouri

Mildred liked to keep several servings on hand in the freezer for guests—or for her own family.

1. Sauté onions, green peppers and celery in margarine over medium heat until translucent, about 5 minutes. Remove from heat.

2. Make a mustard sauce by combining dry mustard, mayonnaise, 2 teaspoons Worcestershire, A-1 and cream; beat well 3 minutes.

3. Combine sautéed vegetables, mustard sauce, crabmeat, 5 cups bread crumbs, milk, Dijon mustard, remaining 1½ teaspoons Worcestershire, salt and white pepper. Mix well.

4. Lightly grease 14 individual baking shells, heat-proof salad plates or ramekins. Divide mixture among the shells (use an ice-cream scoop to make an attractive presentation). Sprinkle each with a scant 1 tablespoon bread crumbs; sprinkle with paprika. Bake at 400 degrees 15 minutes, or until brown.

5. If desired, freeze before baking. When ready to serve, thaw, then bake as usual.

Makes 14 servings

½ cup chopped onion
½ cup chopped green pepper
½ cup chopped celery
¼ cup margarine, melted
5 tsp dry mustard, or to taste
1 cup mayonnaise
3½ tsp Worcestershire sauce, divided
1 tsp A-1 steak sauce
1½ tbsp light cream or half-and-half
¾ pound fresh cooked crabmeat
5½ cups plus 2 tbsp soft bread
   crumbs, divided
¼ cup milk
3 tbsp Dijon mustard
¼ tsp salt
¼ tsp white pepper
Paprika

Spiedini di Gamberi

Donna Birdsong and Michael Staudte, Kansas City, Missouri

2 cloves garlic, peeled and crushed
½ cup olive oil
4 large prawns or jumbo shrimp, peeled and deveined, leaving tails intact
1 tbsp yellow bell pepper cut in very small, thin strips from outermost layer
1 tbsp red bell pepper cut in very small, thin strips from outermost layer
1 tbsp chives or green onions, thinly sliced
4 thin slices prosciutto di Parma, cut in 2-inch-wide strips

Spiedini di Gamberi makes a colorful and flavorful first course.

1. Add garlic to olive oil in ovenproof dish or cup; bake at 200 degrees 30 minutes. Allow to cool to room temperature. Add prawns, yellow pepper, red pepper and chives or green onions. Marinate in refrigerator 1 to 24 hours.

2. Ladle garlic oil onto individual serving plates, making sure each gets all three colors of flavorings (but discard garlic cloves).

3. Grill or broil prawns 5 to 6 minutes, turning once. Prawns will curl, turn opaque and brown lightly.

4. Wrap a slice of prosciutto around the curve of each prawn, and place in garlic-oil on plates.

Note: Other seasonal vegetables may be substituted for the red, yellow and green of the peppers and chives or green onions.

Makes 2 to 4 appetizers

Boiled Green Bananas (*Guineitos Verdesen Escabeche*)

Elvin Ramos, Leavenworth, Kansas

Boiled Green Bananas uses the only fruit that grows well on Elvin's native island of St. Thomas, and they provide the basis for this appetizer or tailgate dish.

1. Make escabeche sauce: In a heavy kettle mix together olive oil, vinegar, peppercorns, ½ teaspoon salt, bay leaves, onions and garlic; cook over low heat 1 hour until onion is tender and flavors are well blended. Allow to cool.

2. For banana layer: Trim bananas at both ends and slit the peel lengthwise on opposite sides. In a deep pot, boil water sufficient to cover bananas. Add bananas, cover and boil slowly over low heat 15 minutes. Drain and peel.

3. Fill the pot with 8 cups water and ½ cup salt and quickly bring to a boil. Add the peeled bananas, cover and boil over low heat 10 minutes. Add 1 more cup water and boil 5 minutes; bananas will be firm but tender. Drain and cool.

4. Cut bananas into 1-inch sections. Place bananas in a deep glass dish. Pour sauce over and stir gently to combine. Marinate 24 hours in refrigerator. Serve cold as an appetizer or main course.

Makes about 30 servings as appetizer or 6 to 8 main course servings

For escabeche sauce:
2 cups olive oil
1 cup vinegar
12 peppercorns
½ tsp salt
2 bay leaves
1½ pounds onions, peeled and sliced
2 cloves garlic, minced

For banana layer:
10 green bananas
9 cups water, divided, plus more for initial boiling
½ cup salt, or to taste

Shrimp and Avocado Appetizer

Paula Murphy, formerly of Leawood, Kansas, now in Pennsylvania

3 tbsp olive oil
2 tbsp white- or red-wine vinegar
1 tsp Dijon mustard
1 pound shrimp, cooked, cleaned
    and cubed
2 tbsp chili sauce, or 1 tsp ground
    chili peppers
1 large clove garlic, crushed
Salt and pepper, to taste
2 tbsp fresh minced dill
2 tbsp fresh chives
1 avocado, peeled, sprinkled with
    lemon juice and diced
½ cup to 1 cup of mayonnaise
Lettuce greens

1. Whisk together olive oil, vinegar and mustard. Combine with shrimp, and marinate 2 hours.

2. Mix chili sauce, garlic, salt, pepper, dill, chives and diced avocado. Drain shrimp. Fold into avocado mixture with enough mayonnaise to blend.

3. Chill. Serve on lettuce greens.

Makes 6 servings

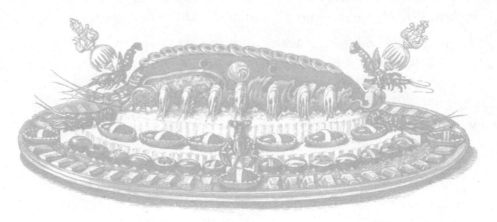

Soups & Salads
For First Courses
& Main Dishes

Soups

Gazpacho

John Taylor, Kansas City, Missouri

4 (16 oz) cans whole peeled
    tomatoes, drained
2 cloves garlic
½ cup olive oil
2 slices bread (any kind)
2 stalks celery with leaves, chopped,
    divided
1 small cucumber, peeled and
    chopped, divided
2 carrots, chopped, divided
1 green pepper, chopped (or use a
    few yellow banana peppers,
    Anaheim chilies; include a fresh
    jalapeno if you like it hot), divided
1 cup shredded purple cabbage,
    divided
1 cup sliced pimento-stuffed olives
1 (3 oz) jar capers, drained
1 fresh tomato, chopped
3 green onions, chopped
2 tbsp chili powder
1 tbsp dried basil
½ cup red wine vinegar, or more to
    taste
Salt to taste
Cottage cheese

This recipe originated with John's mother, Lannie Taylor. John, to his way of thinking, improved on it. Several years ago, unbeknownst to each other, John and Lannie each sent their versions of the recipe to *The Kansas City Star* in response to a reader request. The newspaper printed both.

1. In a blender and working in batches, puree until smooth the canned tomatoes, garlic, oil, bread, half the celery, half the cucumber, half the carrots, half the peppers and half the cabbage. Transfer blended mixture to a large, nonreactive bowl or pitcher.

2. Stir in the second half of celery, cucumber, carrots, peppers and cabbage. Add olives, capers, fresh tomato, green onions, chili powder and basil. Add wine vinegar and salt to taste.

3. Cover and chill overnight. Serve in soup bowls topped with a spoonful of cottage cheese.

Makes 12 to 16 servings

Chilled Creamy Tomato Soup

Robert Barrientos and Marion Broderick, Kansas City, Missouri

This tomato soup recipe makes an excellent leftover—it's even better the second day.

1. Combine all ingredients, except garnish, and mix well.

2. Chill at least 2 hours. Garnish and serve as appetizer or main course, with a green salad and wheat rolls.

Note: You can vary vegetables according to availability, but note that celery tends to overpower other flavors.

Makes 6 servings

1 cucumber, peeled, seeded and chopped
1 green pepper, seeded and chopped
2 green onions, chopped
2 cloves garlic, crushed
1 tsp honey
½ tsp dill weed
4 cups tomato juice
1 cup plain yogurt
Thinly sliced raw mushrooms, watercress sprigs or croutons, for garnish

Melon Soup

Alice Homeyer, Raytown, Missouri

1. Remove cantaloupe pulp, being careful not to use any green flesh near the rind. Puree in food processor.

2. Add orange juice, honey and cream. (If the melon is very ripe and full-flavored, the honey can be omitted. Taste before adding.) Pulse until blended.

3. Serve in glass bowls with a washed nasturtium blossom on top. Or sprinkle cinnamon very lightly on top.

Makes 4 servings

1 large ripe cantaloupe
¼ cup orange juice
¼ cup honey, or to taste
¼ cup cream
Nasturtium blossoms

Main Dish Soups & Stews

Italian Sausage Soup with Tortellini

Danny DiMauro, Kansas City, Missouri

1 pound Italian sausage
1 cup chopped onions
2 garlic cloves, sliced
5 cups beef broth
½ cup water
½ cup good red wine or water
4 medium tomatoes, peeled, seeded
   and chopped
1½ cups thinly sliced carrots
1 tsp fresh minced basil
½ tsp fresh minced oregano
8 ounces tomato sauce
1½ cups zucchini, peeled and sliced
2 cups cheese-filled dry tortellini
   (tricolor is pretty)
3 tbsp chopped fresh parsley
1 medium red or green bell pepper,
   cut in chunks
Grated fresh Parmesan cheese

This Italian sausage soup with tortellini is Danny's own creation, but he is quick to credit his grandmother's soup base as key to its rich and spicy flavor.

1. Remove sausage from casing, then brown and stir in large Dutch oven or pot over medium heat. Remove sausage as it browns and place on paper towels to drain; take care not to let sausage burn.

2. Drain all but 2 tablespoons drippings from pan. Over medium heat, sauté onions and garlic in drippings until onions are soft, 1 to 2 minutes, making sure garlic doesn't brown.

3. Add beef broth, ½ cup water, wine or additional ½ cup water, tomatoes, carrots, basil, oregano and tomato sauce. Bring to a boil, then simmer, uncovered, 30 minutes. Skim fat from soup.

4. Stir in zucchini, tortellini, parsley and peppers. Simmer 35 to 40 minutes, or until tortellini are tender. Serve hot with Parmesan cheese.

Makes 8 servings

E & J Chili

Sandra Kroh, Lenexa, Kansas

Sandra Kroh and her husband, Roger Kroh, enjoy informal entertaining and simple dishes, such as this Cincinnati-style chili.

1. Add ground beef to cold water in a 4-quart pot. Cook on medium, stirring until beef separates to a fine texture. When mixture reaches a boil, reduce heat and boil slowly 30 minutes.

2. Add remaining ingredients, and stir to blend. Bring to a boil. Reduce heat and simmer uncovered about 3 hours, or until flavors are well blended and chili is desired consistency. Pot may be covered the last hour or so after desired consistency is reached.

3. Allow to cool, then refrigerate overnight. Lift accumulated fat off surface, remove bay leaf and cloves and reheat until heated through.

4. Serve with any of the additions.

Makes 8 servings

2 pounds ground beef
1 quart cold water
2 medium onions, finely chopped
2 (8 oz) cans tomato sauce
½ tsp allspice
1½ tsp red pepper
2 tbsp vinegar
5 whole cloves
1½ tsp salt
½ ounce unsweetened chocolate
1 tsp cumin
4 tbsp chili powder
4 cloves garlic, minced
1 bay leaf
2 tsp Worcestershire sauce
1 tsp ground cinnamon

Additions:
Hot cooked spaghetti
Chopped onions
Oyster crackers
Cooked red beans
Grated cheese

Gumbo

Georgia Buchanan, Kansas City, Missouri

For chicken and stock:
1 large hen (about 5 pounds)
1 green pepper, cut in large chunks
1 onion, cut in large chunks
3 stalks celery, cut in large chunks
4 bay leaves

For creole sauce:
1 stalk celery, chopped
4 onions, chopped
1 bunch green onions, chopped
3 cloves garlic
3 green peppers, chopped
1 (16 oz) can tomatoes, cut up
1 (15 oz) can tomato sauce
1 (16 oz) can Italian-style tomatoes
1 (3.25 oz) crab and shrimp boil
   seasoning
1 tbsp Russian salad dressing
1 tbsp Worcestershire Sauce
1 tbsp Tabasco sauce
1 tsp dry mustard
1 tsp chili powder
¼ tsp cayenne
¼ tsp paprika
1 cup all-purpose flour
1 cup vegetable shortening

"People ask me for [the gumbo recipe] all the time," Georgia says. "It's a favorite." Since the recipe takes some time to make, Georgia usually prepares it in parts over a week's time. When she's finished, she immediately freezes the gumbo.

1. In pot, cover chicken with water. Add green pepper, onion, celery and bay leaves. Bring water to boil, reduce to slow boil and cook until tender, 20 to 30 minutes. Do not overcook; chicken will be firm, not stringy. Remove from heat, and let chicken cool in stock.

2. Remove chicken from pot, reserving stock. Discard vegetables. Cut chicken meat into bite-size pieces; discard bones. Return cut-up chicken to stock.

3. For creole sauce: Sauté celery, onions, green onions, garlic and green peppers in skillet in about 1 tablespoon fat from chicken stock or bacon drippings until tender, about 5 minutes.

4. In large pot, put tomatoes, tomato sauce, Italian-style tomatoes, 2 cups of the stock from cooking chicken, crab and shrimp boil bag, Russian dressing, Worcestershire sauce, Tabasco sauce, dry mustard, chili powder, cayenne and paprika. Add sautéed vegetables.

5. In a saucepan over medium heat, stir flour and vegetable shortening and cook just until lightly brown; whisk in 3 to 4 cups chicken stock. Stir into tomato mixture. Cook and stir over medium heat until mixture thickens and bubbles, about 20 minutes.

6. Heat oil in large skillet over medium heat; sauté mushrooms, okra, and water chestnuts 7 to 8 minutes to blend flavors and to cook okra. (This step can be done in advance.) Set aside.

7. Shell and devein shrimp. If large, cut in half or into chunks; leave small shrimp whole.

8. Remove chicken from stock. Bring remaining stock to boil. (If necessary to allow shrimp to move freely in stock, add canned stock to pan.) Add shrimp to stock, and cook just until the shrimp turn pink, 2 to 3 minutes.

9. Stir in chicken, then combine mixture and sausage with the creole sauce. Add sautéed okra, mushrooms and water chestnuts. Add crabmeat. Stir well to combine, and cook just until heated through. Do not overcook.

10. Stir in gumbo file, if desired. Serve over fluffy rice or dry chow mein noodles.

Makes 30 to 40 servings

(Ingredients continued)

Final additions:
1 tbsp vegetable oil
12 ounces canned sliced
   mushrooms, drained
1 (16 oz) package frozen cut okra,
   optional
1 (8 oz) can water chestnuts, diced
5 to 7 pounds fresh shrimp
1 pound smoked sausage, cut into
   bite-size pieces
1 pound fresh crabmeat
Gumbo file, to taste, optional
Rice or chow mein noodles

Yassa

Sandra Dean, Kansas City, Missouri

1 or 2 chickens, cut up, including
      giblets (5 to 6 pounds total), or
      use about 4 pounds chicken parts
4 heads garlic
9 pounds onions
1 cup red wine vinegar
2 fresh chili peppers
Crushed dried chili peppers to taste
1 tbsp black pepper, or to taste
3 tbsp cooking oil, plus more to coat
      pan
6 cups brown or long-grain white rice
Water
Salt, to taste
1 tbsp soy sauce, or to taste

Yassa, a sort of stew from Senegal, traditionally is eaten communally, with each diner having a portion of a large serving bowl. Sandra found the recipe in *African Cooking for Western Kitchens*.

1. Wash chicken pieces and pat dry.

2. Divide the garlic into cloves; crush and peel.

3. In a large stew pot, combine the garlic, onions, vinegar, fresh chili peppers, crushed dry chili peppers and black pepper. Add the chicken pieces. Stir well, cover and marinate in refrigerator several hours or overnight.

4. When ready to prepare: Heat 3 tablespoons oil in large pan over medium-high heat. Remove chicken from marinade, reserving marinade, and fry in oil until brown on all sides. Remove pieces and set aside.

5. Remove onions from marinade, and fry them in the same oil as chicken until onions are light brown and somewhat limp.

6. Return onions and chicken to marinade, and bring mixture to a boil; reduce heat and simmer at least 2 hours, or until chicken is cooked through and flavors are blended. The longer it simmers, the more the flavors develop.

7. Meanwhile, coat the bottom of another large heavy pot with a small amount of oil. Heat over medium-high heat, then lightly fry the rice. Add water: 11½ cups for white rice, or 18 cups for brown rice. Bring to a boil. Cover, reduce heat to low, and cook 30 to 50 minutes, or until rice is tender and water is absorbed.

8. When ready to eat, add salt and soy sauce to chicken mixture. To serve, spread the rice in a wide, flat platter or bowl. Let cool 5 to 10 minutes. Remove chicken pieces from the sauce and distribute evenly over the rice. Pour onions and sauce over the dish as desired.

Makes 8 to 12 servings

Soul Succotash

Louise Ferguson, Kansas City, Missouri

1. Put turkey wings or necks and water in 5-quart pot. Cover and bring to a boil. Reduce heat and simmer, covered, 1½ hours.

2. Meanwhile, wash beans, snap off ends and remove strings. Break each bean into 3 pieces. After turkey has simmered, add beans, onions, salt and pepper. Simmer, covered, 20 minutes.

3. Add potatoes, okra and corn. Simmer until potatoes are tender, about 15 minutes.

4. Check and correct seasoning. Remove meat from bones and return meat to pot, then serve hot.

Makes 8 servings

4 smoked turkey wings (about 1¼ pounds) or 1¼ pounds smoked turkey necks
6 cups water
1 pound fresh green beans
1 medium onion, chopped (about 1 cup)
Salt to taste
Freshly ground black pepper to taste
6 small new potatoes (about 1 pound), washed and quartered
¾ pound okra, trimmed and sliced ½-inch thick, or 1 (10 oz) package frozen sliced okra, defrosted
1 cup frozen corn kernels or corn cut from 4 cobs

Stock Characters Stew

Barbara Lee Fay, Overland Park, Kansas

¾ cup chopped green pepper
6 tbsp finely chopped onion
3 cloves garlic, put through press
3 tbsp cooking oil
3 (16 oz) cans tomatoes, cut up, with
    liquid
3 (8 oz) cans tomato sauce
1½ cups dry red wine
9 tbsp snipped parsley
1½ tsp salt
¾ tsp dried oregano, crushed
¾ tsp dried basil, crushed
Dash of black pepper
3 pounds frozen white fish fillets
    (skinned perch or cod), thawed
3 (4½ oz) cans shrimp, drained
3 (7½ oz) cans minced clams

Barbara is a member of the Missouri Repertory Theatre Guild, a group of volunteers that supports Kansas City's Missouri Rep. About once a year, Barbara helps serve a twilight supper to cast and crew members at the Rep. Not only is it fun, Barbara says, but the theater group appreciates a home-cooked meal. She adapted this recipe from one called Cioppiono Mediterranean, which ran in *Better Homes & Gardens* some 20 years ago.

1. In stockpot, cook green pepper, onion and garlic in oil over medium-high heat until tender but not brown, 5 to 10 minutes.

2. Add tomatoes, tomato sauce, wine, parsley, salt, oregano, basil and black pepper. Bring to a boil. Reduce heat; cover and simmer 40 minutes, or until slightly thickened.

3. Cut fish fillets in bite-size pieces, removing any bones. Add fish to broth; simmer 15 minutes, or until fish is cooked through. Add shrimp and undrained clams; continue simmering, covered, about 10 minutes or until steaming hot (not boiling). Serve hot.

Makes 20 servings

Jambalaya

Tina Fontenot, Kansas City, Missouri

Tina Fontenot is Cajun through and through. Cooking is one way that she keeps her native Louisiana culture alive.

1. Brown sausage in large stockpot, and drain fat.

2. Add cooking oil, yellow onions, bell pepper, garlic and green onions; cook over medium heat until onions are clear, about 10 minutes.

3. Add cajun seasoning and red pepper sauce, water and uncooked rice. Bring to a boil, lower heat to medium, and stir thoroughly. Taste for salt and pepper, and adjust as needed.

4. Cover and cook about ½ hour, or until rice is tender. Consistency should be very moist but not soupy. Serve at once with more red pepper sauce on side.

Note: Tina recommends the andouille sausage at Krizman's House of Sausage in Kansas City, Kansas, as very authentic and "extremely delicious." She also suggests the andouille at Fritz's Smoked Meats in Kansas City, Missouri, and Farmland's Cajun bun sausage as "close to being authentic."

Makes about 15 servings

2 pounds andouille or Polish sausage
3 tbsp cooking oil
2 medium yellow onions, chopped
1 large red bell pepper, chopped
2 tbsp bottled minced garlic
1 cup chopped green onions
1 tbsp Tony Chachere's seasoning, or other cajun seasoning mix
1 tbsp red pepper sauce, plus more as condiment
3 cups water
1½ cups uncooked rice
Salt and ground black pepper to taste

Tomato-Lentil Soup

Mary Honas, Overland Park, Kansas

2 cloves garlic, minced
1 chopped onion
1 tbsp cooking oil
4 cups water
1 cup dried lentils
5 carrots, sliced
2 stalks celery, sliced
3 cups or 1 (28 oz) can tomatoes
1 bay leaf
¾ cup or 1 (6 oz) can tomato paste
2 tbsp parsley flakes
1 tsp thyme leaves
1 tsp dill weed
1 tsp tarragon
1 tsp marjoram

After Mary decided to stay home with her children, she found she used more recipes that took a little more time but called for less expensive ingredients, such as dry beans or lentils. This recipe tastes great with grilled cheese sandwiches.

1. In soup pot, sauté garlic and onion in oil over medium heat until soft, 3 to 4 minutes. Add water and dried lentils; bring to a boil over high, reduce heat to a simmer and cook, covered, until tender, about 45 minutes.

2. Add carrots, celery, tomatoes and bay leaf. Simmer 1 hour.

3. Remove bay leaf. Combine tomato paste, parsley, thyme, dill, tarragon and marjoram. Stir into soup and heat through—and it's ready to serve.

Makes 8 to 10 servings as a main course

Vien's Oxtail Soup

Vivienne A. Smith, Kansas City, Missouri

1. Rinse meat. Place in large soup pot with onion, green pepper, jalapeno pepper, spicy seasoning, black pepper, garlic, bay leaves and water. Bring to a boil over high heat, reduce temperature to low and simmer until meat is tender, about 2 hours.

2. Add the green beans, mixed vegetables, corn and tomato paste. Bring to a boil, reduce heat and simmer another 30 minutes, or until vegetables are tender and flavors have blended.

Makes 8 servings

3 pounds oxtails
1 medium yellow onion
1 medium green pepper
Dried jalapeno pepper (pinch-size piece)
1 tsp Gates Hot & Spicy Seasoning
1/2 tbsp black pepper
1/2 tbsp garlic powder or 2 whole
   cloves garlic
3 medium bay leaves
2 quarts water
1 (16 oz) can green beans
1 (20 oz) package frozen mixed vegetables
1 (16 oz) can whole kernel corn
1 (12 oz) can tomato paste

Black Bean and Vegetable Chili

Charlotte Yates, Lee's Summit, Missouri

This dish is great over cooked rice. You can top it with sour cream or cheese.

1. In a large saucepan over medium heat, cook onion in oil until tender. Add tomatoes, picante sauce, cumin, salt and basil. Cover and simmer 5 minutes.

2. Stir in black beans, green pepper, red pepper and squash; cover and simmer until vegetables are tender, about 15 minutes.

Makes about 8 (1-cup) servings

1 large onion, chopped
1 tbsp vegetable oil
1 (28 oz) can whole tomatoes,
   including juice, chopped
2/3 cup picante sauce
1 1/2 tsp ground cumin
1 tsp salt
1/2 tsp dried basil
1 (16 oz) can black beans, rinsed and drained
1 green bell pepper, chopped
1 red bell pepper, chopped
1 large yellow squash or zucchini,
   cut into 1/2-inch chunks

Cheddar Chowder

Beverly Tibbetts, Lansing, Kansas

2 cups water
2 cups diced potatoes
½ cup diced carrots
½ cup diced celery
¼ cup chopped onions
1 tsp salt
¼ tsp pepper
¼ cup butter
¼ cup all-purpose flour
2 cups milk
2 cups grated cheddar cheese
1 cup cubed ham

"I think my favorite kinds of recipes have been in the family and community for a long time," Beverly says. "I like the feeling of an established recipe, a homey feeling."

1. Combine water, potatoes, carrots, celery, onion, salt and pepper in large kettle. Bring to boil, and cook 10 to 12 minutes, or until vegetables are tender.

2. Meanwhile, in small saucepan, make white sauce: Melt butter over medium heat. Add flour, and stir until smooth, about 1 minute. Slowly add milk, stirring constantly; continue cooking, stirring occasionally, until thickened, 5 to 8 minutes.

3. Add grated cheese to white sauce; stir until melted. Add white sauce and cubed ham to vegetables in their cooking liquid. Heat through, and serve.

Makes 4 servings

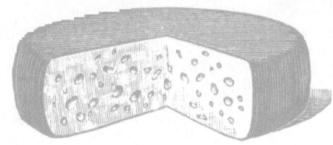

Asian Chicken Salad

Sara Powell, Kansas City, Missouri

Sara likes to try out restaurant flavors at home. This dish is the result of one experiment.

1. Marinate chicken breasts in mesquite marinade about 1 hour.

2. Remove from marinade. Grill chicken over hot coals until cooked through. Cool, then slice chicken into ¼-inch strips.

3. Mix iceberg lettuce, Romaine lettuce, cilantro, green onions and carrots.

4. Make honey-lime vinaigrette: Combine oil, vinegar, honey and lime juice. Mix well. This can be made in advance and refrigerated up to 5 days.

5. Pour vinaigrette over lettuce mixture and toss. Add chicken breasts, and spoon Szechuan peanut sauce over; toss. Top with crumbled tortilla chips.

Makes 4 servings as a main dish

4 boneless chicken breast halves
Mesquite marinade, such as Lawry's
½ head iceberg lettuce, torn into bite-size pieces
1 head Romaine lettuce, torn into bite-size pieces
¼ cup chopped cilantro
5 green onions, including lower third of green tops, finely chopped
1 carrot, shredded

For honey-lime vinaigrette:
½ cup vegetable oil
2 tbsp rice wine vinegar, or white (distilled) vinegar
1 tsp honey
Juice of 2 limes

For topping:
3 tbsp, or to taste, Szechuan peanut sauce, such as Jade brand (available at some specialty shops)
Restaurant-style tortilla chips

Pasta Salad with Spinach Pesto

Leni and Neil Salkind, Lawrence, Kansas

For spinach pesto:
1 (10 oz) package frozen spinach, thawed and moisture squeezed out
1 cup fresh parsley leaves
⅔ cup grated Parmesan cheese
½ cup walnuts
4 flat anchovies
2 cloves garlic, mashed to paste
¼ tsp ground fennel
1 tsp dried basil
1 tsp salt
1 cup olive oil

For pasta salad:
1 medium red bell pepper, optional
1 pound rotini (corkscrew) noodles
2 (10 oz) packages frozen peas, run under cold water to thaw
2 (7 oz) cans tuna, drained
Salt and ground black pepper, to taste

Leni and Neil live without air-conditioning. In a Kansas summer that can mean some hot evenings, so Leni and Neil often choose dishes that can be prepared in the cool mornings. This dish makes a great summer meal, even if you have air-conditioning.

1. To make spinach pesto, place spinach, parsley, Parmesan, walnuts, anchovies, garlic, fennel, basil and salt in food processor; blend. With motor running, add olive oil in a stream (makes 2 cups pesto).

2. To make pasta salad: Blanch red pepper 30 seconds; refresh in cold water, then cut in ½-inch pieces. Cook rotini in pot of boiling salted water until al dente (tender, but firm to the tooth). Drain, rinse in cold water and drain well.

3. In large bowl, combine red pepper, pasta, spinach pesto, thawed peas, tuna and salt and black pepper to taste; serve at room temperature.

Makes 4 to 6 servings

Orange and Fennel Salad

Mary Beth Ricci, Olathe, Kansas

1. Peel oranges, remove white pith and any seeds, then slice.
2. Arrange the orange slices on a platter.
3. Cut fennel bulbs in half lengthwise and then into strips. Distribute the fennel and olives over the oranges.
4. Drizzle with olive oil, and sprinkle with salt and pepper. Toss gently to serve.

3 large navel oranges
2 medium fennel bulbs, leaves and root end trimmed
½ cup dried, cured black kalamata olives
3 tbsp olive oil
Salt and pepper to taste

Makes 4 to 6 servings

Raspberry Salad

Ann Thomas, Prairie Village, Kansas

"I tend to cook things that are different but easy," says Ann.

1. In food processor or blender, blend vinegar, jam and oil; set aside.
2. In bowl, combine lettuce, nuts, raspberries and kiwis. Pour dressing over.
3. Toss well and serve immediately.

3 tbsp raspberry vinegar
3 tbsp raspberry jam
¼ cup canola oil
1 large bunch fresh green leaf lettuce, torn into bite-size pieces
¼ cup chopped macadamia nuts
1 cup fresh raspberries
3 kiwis, peeled and sliced

Note: Raspberries frozen without syrup may be substituted for fresh raspberries.

Makes 6 servings

Green Salad Mold

Geraldine Waanders, Olathe, Kansas

1 (3 oz) package lime-flavored gelatin
¾ cup boiling water
1 medium onion, grated
1½ cups grated or finely chopped and
    seeded cucumber, peeled if desired
1 cup cottage cheese
1 cup nut meats
1 tbsp lemon juice
½ cup mayonnaise
1 tsp salt

Although it "sounds like yuck," Geraldine says, this green salad mold is really very good.

1. Stir gelatin into boiling water until dissolved.

2. Stir remaining ingredients into gelatin; blend well.

3. Pour into 1½-quart mold or 8-inch square pan treated with nonstick cooking spray; chill until firm. Unmold or cut into squares to serve.

Makes about 8 servings

Apple Salad

Chris Cindric, Prairie Village, Kansas

1 Red Delicious apple, cored and
    chopped
1 Golden Delicious or Granny Smith
    apple, cored and chopped
½ cup seedless raisins
½ cup golden raisins
½ cup chopped celery
½ cup cubed cheddar cheese
¼ cup chopped macadamia nuts
Juice of 1 orange
8 ounces vanilla yogurt
Ground cinnamon

1. In medium bowl, combine red apples, golden apples, raisins, golden raisins, celery, cheese and nuts.

2. Blend orange juice into yogurt. Pour over salad and toss well. Sprinkle cinnamon on top and serve.

Makes 8 servings

Celery Salad

Kelly and Billie Bauer, Overland Park, Kansas

1. Cut celery crosswise into ¼-inch slices. Put in bowl. Add red onions.
2. In small bowl, combine remaining ingredients except parsley flakes. Pour over celery and red onions. Toss. Top with parsley flakes.
3. Chill at least 4 hours and serve. Leftovers are great.

Makes about 6 servings

1 bunch celery
1 red onion, cut in 1-inch strips
6 tbsp vegetable oil
2 tbsp red wine vinegar
½ tsp salt
Freshly ground black pepper
2 ounces blue cheese, crumbled
2 green onions, chopped
About 2 tbsp parsley flakes

Two-Bean Supreme Salad

Trish Byall, Leawood, Kansas

This recipe, which can be prepared in advance, is a great serve-yourself dish for a party.

1. Combine green beans, wax beans, olives, mushrooms, artichoke hearts, onions and dressing in bowl. Marinate in refrigerator several hours or overnight; stir occasionally.
2. Just before serving, add sliced cherry tomatoes and Parmesan cheese. Mix well.

Makes 8 to 10 servings

2 (16 oz) cans cut green beans, drained
1 (16 oz) can wax beans, drained
1 (4 oz) can sliced black olives, drained
1 (4 oz) can button mushrooms, drained
2 (6 oz) jars marinated artichoke hearts, including marinade
1 small red onion, thinly sliced
1 cup Italian salad dressing
½ pint cherry tomatoes, sliced
½ cup grated Parmesan cheese

Cole Slaw with Mandarin Oranges

Serese Cannon, Kansas City, Missouri

1 (1-pound) package precut cole slaw vegetables
Mayonnaise-style salad dressing, such as Miracle Whip
1 (11 oz) can mandarin oranges, reserving liquid

1. Shake out cole slaw vegetables into a bowl. Add salad dressing, stirring, to taste or until smooth.

2. Add oranges and liquid, to taste.

Makes 8 to 10 servings

Prospect Salad

Alice Homeyer, Raytown, Missouri

2 large heads butter lettuce
1 bunch parsley, leaves removed and chopped
1 can hearts of palm, drained and sliced crosswise
Seasoned, toasted English walnuts (recipe follows)
½ pound blue cheese, chopped
Prospect Vinaigrette (see recipe on page 46)

The Prospect, in Kansas City's Westport neighborhood, was a popular restaurant for many years before it closed. This salad was a favorite of Prospect fans.

1. Arrange lettuce on plates and sprinkle with parsley.

2. Top each plate with hearts of palm slices, walnuts and blue cheese.

3. Dress to taste with vinaigrette. (You will have a good deal of dressing left over.)

Makes 6 servings

Seasoned, Toasted English Walnuts

Alice Homeyer, Raytown, Missouri

1. Melt butter in mixing bowl in microwave. Add walnuts, and toss to coat with butter.

2. Sprinkle with about half the seasoned salt. Toss to season all walnuts. Taste. Add additional salt to taste. Toss.

3. Spread walnuts in a single layer on a baking sheet. Bake at 250 degrees until crisp, about 1 hour. (Bite into a nut to determine crispness.) Every 15 minutes, stir and turn to ensure even roasting.

4. Cool on baking pan. Store in air-tight container.

Makes 3 cups

1/4 pound butter
3 cups English walnuts
1 1/4 tsp seasoned salt, or to taste

Endive and Roquefort Salad

Pat and Larry Lillis, Kansas City, Missouri

1. Wash and separate the endive leaves and pat dry. Place the leaves, walnuts and crumbled cheese in a large salad bowl.

2. Prepare dressing: Combine 1/2 teaspoon salt and lemon juice in small bowl; stir to blend. Add oil, stirring to blend. Pour over salad ingredients, and toss well.

3. Add salt and pepper to taste.

Makes 6 servings

2 pounds Belgian endive
1 cup walnut pieces
6 ounces French Roquefort
1/2 tsp salt
4 tbsp lemon juice
1/2 cup walnut oil
Salt and pepper to taste

Olive Salad

Kay Ludecke, Overland Park, Kansas

1 (32 oz) jar broken, pimento-stuffed
   green olives
6 cloves garlic, minced
1 (7 oz) jar marinated cocktail onions
   (1 cup), drained
4 stalks celery, cut in half lengthwise
   and thinly sliced
2 tbsp drained capers
1 tbsp dried oregano
1 tsp finely ground black pepper
3 tbsp red wine vinegar
⅓ cup olive oil

"I love to entertain," Kay says, "and when I entertain, I feed people."

1. Drain olives, reserving 3 tablespoons brine. In medium bowl, combine olives, garlic, onions, celery and capers.

2. In a small bowl, whisk together reserved olive brine, oregano, pepper and vinegar. Add olive oil in a slow, steady stream, whisking constantly. Pour dressing over salad; toss.

3. Spoon mixture into jar with a tight-fitting lid. Refrigerate until ready to serve, up to 3 weeks. Serve at room temperature.

Makes about 5 cups

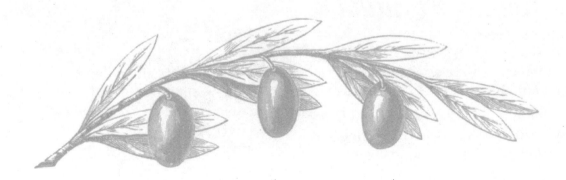

Roasted New Potatoes with Mustard and Watercress Dressing

Lisa Curran, Kansas City, Missouri

Lisa Curran appreciates recipes that allow her to serve delicious and beautiful food and that can be made in advance. This dish meets all the requirements.

1. Place rack in center of oven, and preheat oven to 375 degrees. Oil a large heavy baking pan, such as a 9- by 13-inch casserole dish.

2. Mix 6 tablespoons oil, garlic, salt, pepper, thyme and rosemary in large bowl. Add potatoes and toss by hand to coat. Transfer mixture to prepared pan, spreading potatoes across pan bottom.

3. Bake, stirring occasionally, until potatoes are tender and golden brown, about 55 minutes. Cool.

4. Transfer potatoes to bowl. Scrape pan drippings into measuring cup. Add enough olive oil to drippings to measure 6 tablespoons.

5. Whisk vinegar and mustard together in small bowl. Gradually whisk in oil mixture. Mix in shallots. Pour dressing over potatoes and toss to combine. Season to taste with salt and pepper.

6. Let stand 1 hour at room temperature. (Can be prepared 6 hours ahead; let stand at room temperature.)

7. Add watercress to potatoes, and toss to coat. Mound salad on a platter.

Makes 6 servings

About 11 tbsp olive oil, divided
5 to 6 large cloves garlic, according to taste, chopped
1 tsp salt
1/2 tsp freshly ground black pepper
1/2 tsp dry thyme leaves, crumbled
1/4 tsp dry rosemary, crumbled
2 1/2 pounds medium-size red new potatoes (about 10), scrubbed and cut into 1/2-inch-thick slices
2 tbsp white wine vinegar
2 tbsp Dijon mustard
1/4 cup finely chopped shallots
1 cup watercress tops

Curried Rice Salad

Donna Jacobsen, Kansas City, Missouri

3¾ cups water
2 cups uncooked basmati rice
⅓ cup peanut oil, or to taste
¼ cup lemon juice, or to taste
2 tsp salt
1 tbsp curry powder
1 tsp ground coriander
½ tsp ground black pepper
Pinch cayenne
½ cup dried black currants, soaked
   about 5 minutes in hot water
½ cup shelled pistachio nuts, toasted
4 to 6 green onions, including about
   2 inches of tender green part,
   sliced and, if desired, toasted

Donna Jacobsen's vegetarian dishes are in demand at school potluck meals.

1. Bring water to boil in heavy 2-quart saucepan over high heat. Stir in rice. Return to boil, reduce heat to low, cover and simmer 15 to 20 minutes, until rice is tender and water is absorbed.

2. Combine oil, lemon juice, salt, curry powder, coriander, black pepper and cayenne. Pour dressing over warm rice. Stir in currants, pistachios and green onions.

3. Chill, and serve cold.

Note: Basmati rice is a delicately scented white rice, available in health food stores and some specialty food stores and supermarkets.

Makes 4 to 6 servings

Potato Salad

Diane Marshall, Overland Park, Kansas

Diane's brother-in-law once asked for this recipe to serve for some special guests at Westminster College in Fulton, Missouri. The guests were former Soviet president Mikhail Gorbachev and his wife, Raisa. Diane's brother-in-law, an official at the college, wanted to serve a typical midwestern lunch to the Gorbachevs. The request posed a problem for Diane: "It's one of those things you make till it looks right," she says. The result was a hit, and we're sure you'll like it as much as the Gorbachevs did.

1. Boil potatoes until tender, but not soft. Cool and cube.

2. In large bowl, combine potatoes with eggs, celery, green pepper, radishes, red onions, green onions, cucumbers, olives and gherkin.

3. Combine dressing ingredients. Mix with salad, stirring gently to coat.

Makes 16 servings

5 pounds red potatoes, peeled and quartered
4 hard-cooked eggs
4 stalks celery, chopped
1 green pepper, chopped
1 bunch radishes, chopped
¼ cup red onion, chopped
5 green onions, sliced
1½ cups chopped cucumber
¼ cup chopped green olives
1 small sweet gherkin, minced

Dressing:
2 cups mayonnaise
1 cup sour cream
2 tsp celery salt
Salt and black pepper to taste

Chicken Antipasto Salad

Kathy Miller, Olathe, Kansas

½ cup olive oil
⅓ cup red wine vinegar
2 tbsp fresh minced basil, or 1 tsp dry
     basil
1 tbsp fresh minced parsley
1 clove garlic, minced
1 tsp sugar
3 chicken breast halves, cooked and
     cut into bite-size pieces
1 (14 oz) can artichoke hearts,
     drained and chopped
8 ounces shredded mozzarella
     cheese
1 tomato, diced
1 cucumber, diced
1 cup sliced fresh mushrooms
½ cup salad olives
1 green bell pepper, chopped
2 to 3 green onions, chopped
Salt and ground black pepper, to taste
Lettuce leaves

This antipasto salad came from Kathy's mother.

1. In large bowl, combine oil, vinegar, basil, parsley, garlic and sugar; set aside while cutting remaining ingredients. Add all other ingredients; toss.

2. Serve on lettuce leaves.

Note: If making a day ahead, omit cheese until ready to serve.

Makes 6 servings

New Potato and Snow Pea Salad

Jane Warmbrodt, Fairway, Kansas

1. Steam potatoes over salted water 15 minutes, or until tender. Rinse potatoes under cold water until lukewarm. Drain and set aside.

2. Place lettuce leaves in medium bowl. Drizzle half the vinegar and half the oil over lettuce. Add chives, salt and pepper; toss to combine.

3. Distribute dressed lettuce evenly among 4 to 6 salad plates. Place potatoes in the same medium bowl used for lettuce. Add snow peas, remaining vinegar, remaining oil, salt and pepper; toss gently. Taste for seasoning. Top lettuce with dressed potato mixture.

Note: Salad can be served in one large bowl. Line bowl with the dressed lettuce leaves and place potato mixture over lettuce.

Makes 4 to 6 servings

12 very small (about 1½ inches) new potatoes, scrubbed
1 small head red leaf lettuce, washed and dried
1½ tbsp balsamic vinegar, divided
1½ tbsp olive oil, divided
2 tsp chopped fresh chives
Salt and freshly ground black pepper to taste
1 cup fresh snow peas, washed and trimmed

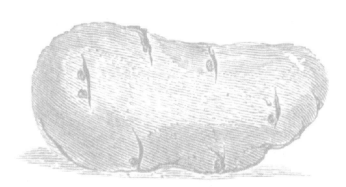

Dressings

Prospect Vinaigrette

Alice Homeyer, Raytown, Missouri

1 cup white vinegar
¼ cup sugar
½ tsp garlic powder
Salt and pepper to taste
2 cups peanut or canola oil

1. Combine all ingredients, except 2 cups oil. Whisk.

2. Add oil in a stream, whisking all the while. Store in covered jar. Shake before using.

Makes about 3 cups

Tarragon Dressing

Lea Hopkins, Leawood, Kansas

1 (½ oz) jar tarragon leaves
1 (5 oz) bottle Worcestershire sauce
1 tsp Tabasco sauce
1 tsp ground white pepper
1 tbsp salt
Leaves from 2 sprigs parsley
1 medium onion, quartered
4 ounces red wine vinegar
1 cup chicken consomme
1 pint vegetable oil
1 quart mayonnaise

1. Place tarragon, Worcestershire, Tabasco, white pepper, salt, parsley leaves, onion and vinegar in blender and mix on high to blend.

2. With motor running, slowly add the consomme and oil. When the mixture reaches a consistency similar to hollandaise sauce, remove from blender and pour into a large mixing bowl.

3. Slowly add the mayonnaise, beating constantly with a wire whisk. Chill and serve with salad.

Makes 1½ quarts

Main Dishes
Meat, Poultry, Seafood & Vegetarian Dishes

Beef, Pork & Lamb

Mock Duck

Mike Mitko, Kansas City, Missouri

2 to 3 pounds round steak
¼ cup plus 2 tbsp all-purpose flour, divided
½ tbsp ground black pepper
½ tsp paprika
½ tsp ground mustard
1½ tbsp ground sage
¼ tsp garlic powder
¼ tsp salt
Dressing (recipe follows)
4 tbsp olive oil
1 (10.5 oz) can condensed tomato soup
1 cup beef stock
½ cup chopped white onion

Mike learned to make Mock Duck from his father—who learned it from his mother-in-law. This unusual dish is an economical cut of round steak, stuffed and shaped to resemble a duck.

1. Trim fat from edges of steak. Mix together ¼ cup flour, pepper, paprika, ground mustard, sage, garlic powder and salt. Sprinkle steak with mixture; pound with meat mallet on both sides until tissue is broken down.

2. Spread dressing over steak; it will make a layer about 1½ inches thick. Roll loosely and tie with kitchen twine in shape of a duck. Remove any dressing that comes out.

3. In a large skillet over high heat, heat olive oil. Sear Mock Duck on all sides, and place in covered baking dish.

4. Stir remaining 2 tbsp flour into oil remaining in skillet. Whisk in condensed tomato soup and beef stock. Add onions. Cook until slightly thickened and bubbling. Pour over Mock Duck and bake, covered, at 300 degrees for 1½ hours, until stuffing is firm.

Makes 4 servings

Dressing for Mock Duck

Mike Mitko, Kansas City, Missouri

1. Sauté onions in olive oil over medium-high heat until translucent. Drain.
2. Combine onions with crumbs, sage, salt, egg, butter, paprika and apples in a bowl. Add enough beef stock to moisten so mixture holds together but isn't wet.

Makes about 2 cups

1 cup chopped onion
3 tbsp olive oil
1½ cups dry corn bread crumbs
2 tsp fresh minced sage leaves
¼ tsp salt
1 egg, beaten
¼ cup melted butter
⅛ tsp paprika
½ cup chopped, peeled tart apples
Beef stock to moisten

Venison Pot Roast

Ron and Barb Thiewes, Kansas City, Missouri

1. Combine herbs and flour; sprinkle part of mixture over all sides of roast. Reserve remaining mixture.
2. Heat oil on medium-high in ovenproof Dutch oven. When hot, brown venison on all sides. Add water and wine, onion and remaining herb-flour mixture. Stir and heat until boiling.
3. Remove from heat; cover and bake at 350 degrees 1½ hours.
4. Add potatoes, carrots and celery. Continue baking until vegetables are tender, about 45 minutes. Season to taste with salt and pepper.

Makes 8 servings

1 cup combination fresh thyme, tarragon, Italian parsley and marjoram leaves
⅓ cup all-purpose flour
3-pound venison roast
3 tbsp olive oil
1 cup water plus ½ cup dry red wine, or 1½ cups water
½ large onion, sliced
1 quart combination of bite-size potato, carrot and celery pieces
Salt and ground black pepper, to taste

Garlic-Stuffed Grilled London Broil

John Bellome, Lenexa, Kansas

¼ cup peeled and finely chopped
   garlic
2 tbsp extra-virgin olive oil
½ cup thinly sliced green onions
½ tsp salt
½ tsp pepper
¼ cup minced parsley
1 (2½- to 3-pound) flank steak
   (London broil), 2 inches thick

Experimentation is a favorite aspect of cooking for John, "much to the dismay of my children," he says.

1. Cook garlic in oil in a small frying pan over low heat until tender, about 5 minutes.

2. Add onions; increase heat to medium-low and continue to cook until onions are tender, about 5 minutes. Stir in salt, pepper and parsley. Remove from heat, and cool thoroughly.

3. With a long, sharp knife, create a pocket in the meat by cutting a slit horizontally through the center, parallel to the surface. Cut to but not through the opposite side. Spoon cooled stuffing into pocket, spreading evenly. Secure opening with toothpicks.

4. Place a lightly greased grill 4 to 6 inches above coals lightly covered with ash. Lay meat on grill. Turn steak as needed to char evenly; cook until a thermometer inserted into thickest part registers 135 degrees for rare (meat is still red in center; cut to test), 12 to 15 minutes per side, or until to desired doneness.

5. Slice meat through filling, removing toothpicks from each portion.

Makes 6 to 8 servings

Cabbage Rolls

Barbara Molinaro, Cleveland, Missouri

These cabbage rolls are based on a recipe Barbara learned from her mother-in-law. They freeze well.

1. In bowl, combine beef, salt, black pepper, 1 clove garlic, 1 tablespoon red pepper, parsley, Parmesan and rice; mix well.

2. Core cabbage. Place cabbage, top down, in boiling water to cover and cook until leaves are tender, about 15 minutes. Peel leaves from head; cut out middle spine of each leaf. Lay each leaf flat and place about ¼ cup of meat mixture on edge of leaf; roll up, tucking in ends.

3. Place cabbage rolls side by side in layers in bottom of a large, heavy Dutch oven. Pour tomato juice, or combination of canned tomatoes and tomato juice, over rolls, covering completely. Season juice to taste with red pepper flakes, salt, black pepper, remaining clove garlic and sugar.

4. Simmer partly covered on top of stove 2½ to 3 hours, or until cooked through and rice is tender. Watch to make sure liquid doesn't boil away; add more tomato juice if necessary.

5. Serve with a salad and crusty bread.

Note: Leftover cabbage and sauce make a great base for steak soup.

Makes 8 servings

2 pounds ground beef
Salt and ground black pepper, to taste
2 garlic cloves, crushed, divided
1 tbsp red pepper flakes, plus more for sauce
1 tsp parsley flakes
3 tbsp Parmesan cheese
½ cup uncooked white rice
1 large head cabbage
2 (46 oz) cans tomato juice, or 2 quarts canned tomatoes with liquid and 1 (46 oz) can tomato juice
1 tbsp sugar

Herb-Scented Tenderloin with Mustard Caper Sauce

Nancy Rieger, Prairie Village, Kansas

1 (4-pound) beef tenderloin butt,
    trimmed of all fat
3 tbsp olive oil
8 branches fresh marjoram or
    oregano, or ¼ cup crumbled
    dried leaves
Mustard Caper Sauce (recipe follows)

1. Rub all sides of tenderloin with oil.

2. Light charcoal and burn until gray ash forms. Spread charcoal in overlapping layers, and let burn 15 minutes. Set grill 3 inches above coals. Set beef on grill and cook about 8 minutes.

3. Turn and continue cooking, frequently sprinkling coals with herbs. Cook until meat thermometer inserted in thickest part of meat registers 135 degrees (medium-rare), or to desired doneness. Remove and let cool.

4. When ready to serve, slice meat thinly and overlap slices on platter. Spoon ribbon of Mustard Caper Sauce down center.

Makes 6 to 8 servings

Mustard Caper Sauce

¼ cup coarsely ground French mustard
2 egg yolks, at room temperature
1 small green onion, chopped
¼ tsp chopped fresh marjoram, or
    pinch of crumbled dried marjoram
Juice of ½ large lemon, about 2 tbsp
1 cup light olive oil, at room temperature
⅓ cup whipping cream
1½ tbsp capers, rinsed and drained

1. Combine mustard, egg yolks, green onion, marjoram and lemon juice in food processor; mix until pale and creamy. With machine running, gradually add oil through feed tube in thin stream, stopping machine occasionally to be sure oil is absorbed.

2. Add cream and capers and mix until blended. Sauce can be prepared up to 3 days ahead and chilled.

Makes about 1½ cups

Sage-Stuffed Beef Tenderloin

Dennis Varble, Kansas City, Missouri

"I cook because I enjoy it, and it's so much different from what I do during the day," says Dennis, who is an architect and construction manager. Dennis adapted a recipe he found in *The Silver Palate Good Times Cookbook* **to arrive at this one.**

1. Preheat oven to 425 degrees. Split tenderloin from end to end, cutting through about ⅔ of the meat's thickness, leaving ⅓ intact. Lay open tenderloin; flatten slightly with meat mallet.

2. Apply thin layer of mustard to cut face of beef. Scatter green peppercorns over and press into meat.

3. Combine ground mixed peppercorns and allspice; sprinkle half the mixture over mustard and green peppercorns. Add a layer of 12 to 16 sage leaves down the middle.

4. Close tenderloin and tie with string. Coat outside with butter, sprinkle with remaining pepper-allspice mixture. Slip bay leaves under string along seam. Place tenderloin on rack in shallow roasting pan.

5. Cover and bake 45 minutes (rare), basting often with melted butter, or to desired doneness.

6. Remove from oven and let stand 10 minutes. Remove bay leaves, slice crosswise, arrange on platter and spoon drippings over meat.

Makes 6 to 8 servings

3 pounds beef tenderloin, trimmed
3 tbsp Dijon-style mustard
1 tbsp water-packed green peppercorns, drained
2½ tbsp ground mixed peppercorns
½ tbsp ground allspice
Fresh sage leaves, about ½ package
2 tbsp butter, plus melted butter for basting
4 bay leaves

Pepper Steak with Smoked Morel Sauce

Steve and Vicki Williams, Roeland Park, Kansas

⅓ cup smoked, dried morel
    mushrooms
4 fillets of beef tenderloin
1 tsp salt
3 tbsp peppercorns, coarsely crushed
3 tbsp butter, plus additional for
    coating pan
1 tbsp extra-virgin olive oil
¼ cup bourbon

Steve and Vicki are lucky to have their own source for morel mushrooms each spring. When the time is ripe, they take off work to gather morels. They wind up with so many that they have developed a way to smoke and dry the mushrooms for reconstitution, which means you can find morels year-round at the Williams house.

1. Soak mushrooms in water to cover 30 minutes. Drain; squeeze out liquid, reserving liquid.

2. Rub steaks with salt. Sprinkle with crushed peppercorns, and use meat mallet to gently pound pepper into both sides of steak.

3. Heat butter and oil in heavy cast-iron skillet over medium-high heat. Add steaks and cook 4 to 8 minutes per side, depending on thickness and desired doneness. Transfer to a warm platter.

4. If necessary, add additional butter to pan so that thin film of grease covers bottom of pan. Add drained morels, bourbon and about 3 tablespoons of reserved morel liquid to deglaze pan. Boil about 1 minute, until slightly reduced.

5. Pour sauce over steaks, and serve.

Makes 4 servings

Involtini di Vitella
(Stuffed Veal Bundles)

Vicki Cali, Kansas City, Missouri

Vicki makes a point to get ingredients for Italian dishes at Scimeca's Grocery, the venerable market in Kansas City's historic Northeast area.

1. Pound veal slices until very thin.

2. Chop provolone and prosciutto into bite-size pieces; add parsley, Romano cheese, pepper and optional garlic powder.

3. Lay one piece of veal flat, and put a heaping tablespoon of cheese mixture on top (do not use so much filling that it will fall out of rolled-up veal). Roll up filled veal slice, and tie with string or fasten with toothpicks. Repeat with the other veal slices.

4. Dredge veal rolls in flour to coat lightly. Heat olive oil in skillet over medium heat, and sauté veal rolls until golden brown, about 15 minutes. Remove bundles from pan, and salt if desired.

5. Stir wine into pan drippings over medium heat. Stir constantly until thickened, and sauce is golden. Remove string or toothpicks from veal bundles, pour wine sauce over bundles and serve.

Makes 4 servings

4 thin slices veal
3 to 4 slices provolone cheese, about ¼ pound
3 to 4 slices prosciutto, about ¼ pound
1½ tbsp minced parsley, or parsley flakes
¼ cup grated Romano cheese, or Parmesan cheese
1 tsp coarsely ground pepper
¼ tsp garlic powder, optional
¼ cup all-purpose flour
2 tbsp olive oil
Salt, optional
¾ cup dry white wine

Yugoslavian Djuvie

Marjorie Mayes, Kansas City, Missouri

5 medium onions, thinly sliced
¼ cup vegetable oil
1 pound cubed pork
5 ripe tomatoes, sliced ½-inch thick
Salt and ground black pepper
1 cup fresh green beans, cut into
   pieces
2 cups peeled, diced eggplant
2 cups diced green pepper
1 carrot, peeled and sliced about
   ¼-inch thick
½ cup uncooked rice (not instant)
1 cup water
Salt and ground black pepper, to taste

The long cooking time for Yugoslavian Djuvie, a recipe Marjorie got from a friend, works nicely when entertaining a large group. This dish is practically a meal in itself.

1. Preheat oven to 375 degrees. Lightly oil a 9- by 13-inch baking pan.

2. In skillet over medium-high heat, sauté onions in oil until soft but not brown. Remove onions from skillet and set aside. Add pork to skillet and brown; remove from heat.

3. Arrange half the onions on bottom of baking dish. Top with half the tomatoes. Sprinkle with salt and pepper. Add layers of half the green beans, half the eggplant, half the green peppers and half the carrots. Top with all the rice and pork. Season with salt and pepper to taste.

4. Add in layers remaining onions, tomatoes, green beans, eggplant, green peppers and carrots. Sprinkle with salt and pepper to taste.

5. Swirl water in skillet, then pour over all. Cover and bake 2½ hours. Uncover and bake 30 minutes more.

Makes 10 to 12 servings

Fyldt Stegt Suine Kam (Danish Stuffed Pork Loin)

Sharon McDaniel, Lee's Summit, Missouri

A Danish-style meal of braised cabbage, roasted potatoes and Stuffed Pork Loin has become a Christmas tradition for Sharon and her family.

1. Untie and unroll pork loin. Sprinkle apples with lemon juice. Lay apples and prunes along length of meat. Tightly reroll fruit and loin, and tie. Preheat oven to 350 degrees.

2. Melt butter and heat oil in heavy, ovenproof pan over medium-high heat. Brown loin evenly on all sides, about 20 minutes. Remove meat from pan and set aside.

3. Drain fat from pan. Pour in wine and briskly whisk in heavy cream. Bring just to a simmer, and return meat to pan.

4. Cover pan and place in center of oven 1 hour 30 minutes. Remove pan from oven. Remove loin from pan; keep warm. Skim fat from pan juices.

5. Bring remaining liquid to a boil on top of stove. Reduce to 1 cup, then stir in jelly. Reduce heat; simmer, stirring constantly, until sauce is smooth. Season with salt and pepper, and serve hot on side with sliced pork.

Makes 6 to 8 servings

1 (5-pound) boned pork loin, center-cut
1 large tart apple, peeled, cored and cut into 1-inch pieces
1 tsp lemon juice
12 medium pitted prunes, cooked according to package directions
3 tbsp butter
3 tbsp vegetable oil
¾ cup dry white wine

¾ cup heavy cream

1 tbsp red currant jelly
Salt and freshly ground pepper, to taste

Orange Glazed Pork Roast

Elsie Ball, Leawood, Kansas

3 tbsp all-purpose flour
10- by 16-inch oven roasting bag
2 tsp instant chicken bouillon
1 tsp ground cinnamon
1¼ cups orange juice
2½ to 3 pounds boneless pork loin
    roast
¾ tsp thyme
Salt and pepper, to taste

1. Shake flour into roasting bag. Place bag in 13- by 9- by 2-inch baking pan. Add the chicken bouillon, cinnamon and orange juice to bag. Squeeze bag to blend ingredients.

2. Rub pork with thyme, salt and pepper. Place in bag, fat side up. Close bag with tie. Make six (½-inch) slits in top of bag.

3. Bake 1 to 1½ hours at 325 degrees, or until meat thermometer inserted in center registers 170 degrees. Remove pork from bag. Stir sauce from bag, and spoon over roast.

Note: Two (1-pound) pork tenderloins may be substituted for the roast. Tie tenderloins together with string before placing in bag. Cooking time will be 45 minutes to 1 hour, or until meat thermometer inserted in center of meat registers 170 degrees.

Makes 6 to 8 servings

Spicy Salsa Steaks

Andrea Duncan, Kansas City, Missouri

4 small rib eye steaks, 1 inch thick
1 cup salsa
¼ cup fresh lime juice
3 tbsp vegetable oil
½ cup chopped cilantro
1 tsp cumin
3 cloves garlic, crushed
Red pepper flakes, to taste

1. Place steaks in a shallow dish in a single layer. Do not overlap. In a mixing bowl, combine remaining ingredients. Pour mixture over the steaks.

2. Cover and marinate in refrigerator overnight.

3. Prepare coals in grill. When coals are hot, remove steaks from marinade and grill to desired doneness.

Makes 4 servings

Nadlava

Jean Cindric, Kansas City, Kansas

Nadlava is a Croatian specialty for Easter. Jean got the recipe from her husband's sister. "It takes a long time to make," Jean says, "but it's worth it."

1. Combine ham, bread, eggs, green onions, pepper and bacon. Let sit ½ hour.

2. Soak casings in warm water 10 minutes to soften.

3. Fill casing with ham mixture, holding one end of casing closed with one hand and packing tightly with spoon. Hit filled casing firmly against counter to remove air pockets; tie ends with string. Prick casing in several places with tip of paring knife. Place on baking sheet.

4. Bake at 300 degrees 1 hour 15 minutes.

Nadlava is usually served cold and sliced.

Note: Casings can be purchased at a butcher's. Typically, Jean buys 2 casings 4 inches in diameter, and cuts them to the desired length.

Makes 30 or more servings

4 pounds smoked ham, cut into ¼-inch cubes
1 (16 oz) loaf bread, cut into ½-inch cubes
15 eggs, beaten
2 bunches green onions, including tender green tops, cut very thin
½ tsp black pepper
1 pound bacon, uncooked, cut very fine
3 (4-inch by 2-foot) casings

Sausage Mushroom Tunnels

David German and Dirick Matteson, Gladstone, Missouri

1½ pounds Italian sausage
24 ounces spaghetti sauce
1 tbsp ground oregano
1 tbsp cajun seasoning
½ medium yellow onion, diced
1 tbsp garlic powder
½ pound fresh mushrooms, sliced
½ tbsp Parmesan cheese
6 ounces red wine
6 unsliced Italian hoagie rolls (about
    3 by 8 inches)
1½ pounds grated mozzarella cheese

David and Dirick are sports fans who like to cook up delicious meals and snacks with whatever they find in Dave's kitchen or looks good at the grocery. Food to watch football by is a specialty.

1. Brown sausage in skillet over medium heat; drain and set aside.

2. In a medium saucepan, combine all ingredients except hoagie rolls and mozzarella cheese. Bring to a boil over medium-high heat, reduce heat and simmer, partly covered, about 30 minutes to blend flavors.

3. Meanwhile, cut ¾ inch off the end of each hoagie and save. Using a serrated knife, carefully hollow out hoagies, leaving about ½-inch bread all the way around, being careful not to puncture or cut the shell. Discard the crumbs from center or save for another use.

4. Fill the bread in alternating layers with mozzarella and sauce. Start with about 2 tablespoons mozzarella, and pack it to the bottom. Next, add about 2 tablespoons sauce, holding the roll upright, and tapping bottom on counter to settle the sauce. Repeat until full, but don't overstuff or hoagie will split. Place the end of the roll backward into the opening (heel end first).

5. Place filled hoagies in 9- by 13- by 3-inch baking pan. Top with remaining sauce and cheese. Bake uncovered at 350 degrees until cheese is melted and golden brown, about 30 minutes. Scoop each bun onto a plate and serve hot.

Note: Dish tastes best with sausage that is not extremely salty.

Makes 6 servings

Spaghetti and Meatballs

Marie Cacioppo, Kansas City, Missouri

Marie edited the 1992 edition of *American Daughters of Columbus Cook Book*. She also contributed recipes to the book.

1. For meatballs: In large bowl, combine all meatball ingredients with hands. Wet palms of hands, and shape mixture into balls about 1½ inches across. (Makes about 17 meatballs.)

2. Heat oil in skillet over medium heat, and fry meatballs, turning occasionally, until golden brown. Remove balls from skillet, and set aside.

3. For sauce: Strain meatball drippings into large saucepan over medium heat; sauté 2 cloves garlic and onion. Add tomato puree, tomato paste and water (use some of the water to get all the tomato paste out of cans). Stir until well blended.

4. Add sugar and seasonings. Let come to a rolling boil; lower heat and simmer, uncovered, over low heat 1 hour 30 minutes.

5. Add meatballs to sauce. Simmer 1 hour more. Stir occasionally. If sauce gets too thick, gradually add a little warm water.

6. Cook spaghetti according to package directions, and serve topped with sauce and meatballs.

Makes 6 servings

For meatballs:
1 pound ground chuck
1 cup bread crumbs
½ cup grated Parmesan or Romano cheese
1 clove garlic, finely minced
Salt and pepper, to taste
¼ pound ground pork
4 eggs, beaten
¼ cup minced parsley
⅓ cup warm water
¼ cup oil or shortening

For sauce:
Drippings from meatballs
2 cloves garlic, minced
1 onion, chopped
1 (24 oz) can tomato puree
3 (6 oz) cans tomato paste
6 cups water
2 tbsp sugar, or to taste
½ tsp dried basil
Dash of red pepper, optional
Salt and pepper, to taste
1½ pounds spaghetti

Stuffed Zucchini

Sammy Ayyad, Kansas City, Missouri

3 pounds (12 to 14) zucchini, up to 6
    inches long (make sure zucchini
    are straight)
1½ tbsp salt plus 2 tsp, divided
2 tbsp butter
¼ small onion, chopped
1 cup long-grain white rice
1 pound lamb shoulder, finely
    chopped
Ground black pepper, to taste
3 medium tomatoes, peeled, or 1
    (1-pound) can stewed tomatoes
Olive oil, about 2 tbsp

Sammy's favorite cooking revolves around re-creating Middle Eastern dishes, particularly Palestinian dishes, and he relishes the task. "Stuffed Zucchini is the best dish of my life!" he says. "I love it!"

1. Slice off stem end of zucchini. Core zucchini using Arabic coring tool *(mikwarah)*, vegetable peeler or long straight-bladed knife. Leave ¼-inch walls, and be careful not to pierce skin. Add 1 tablespoon salt to a pan of cold water; rinse zucchini in salted water, and drain.

2. Melt butter in large saucepan or deep skillet over medium heat. Sauté onion until tender, about 4 minutes; set aside. Meanwhile, rinse rice well and drain, then place in a bowl. Add lamb, ½ tablespoon salt (or to taste) and pepper. Mix well.

3. If you like tomato in stuffing, dice half the tomatoes fine and add to meat; otherwise, slice tomatoes and set aside.

4. Sprinkle rice mixture with olive oil and mix well. Using fingers, stuff zucchini ¾ full, gently tamping filling, or to about 1 inch from end, to allow for expansion of rice.

5. Arrange zucchini over sautéed onion in skillet. Place remaining (or all) tomatoes on top. Barely cover with water and sprinkle with remaining 2 teaspoons salt. Cover and cook on medium heat about 35 minutes, or until rice is tender. Gently remove zucchini to serving platter.

6. Serve cooking liquid in pitcher to be poured over zucchini and filling.

7. Waiting 5 to 10 minutes after cooking to serve will make the zucchini easy to handle with fingers or fork. Serve 2 to 3 zucchini per person.

Note: Ground chuck, chicken or turkey may be substituted for lamb.

Makes 6 to 8 servings

Italian Tomato-Sausage Sauce

Curt Stokes, Kansas City, Kansas

This tomato-sausage sauce is versatile. Curt waits till tomatoes are inexpensive and plentiful, then makes large batches of the sauce and freezes it.

1. In a large saucepan, heat oil over high heat. Add sausage, reduce heat to medium, and cook until meat is no longer pink, taking care not to overcook.

2. Add shallots and garlic; cook 1 minute. Add tomatoes, Italian herbs and sugar. Bring to a fast boil, then simmer uncovered 40 minutes. Stir frequently and skim off fat.

3. Add salt and pepper to taste. Excellent for lasagna or spaghetti.

Note: Canned tomatoes may be substituted for fresh. In that case, omit the 1/2 teaspoon sugar.

Makes 6 servings

2 tbsp extra-virgin olive oil
2 pounds Italian sausage, casings removed, meat crumbled
2 shallots, finely chopped
1 large clove garlic, finely chopped
2 pounds fresh plum tomatoes, processed through a food mill
2 tbsp Italian herbs, or combination of basil, oregano and rosemary
1/2 tsp sugar
1 tsp salt, or to taste
1/8 tsp ground black pepper

Spaghetti Pie

Jo Ann Butler, Kansas City, Missouri

6 ounces cut spaghetti or elbow
  macaroni, cooked according to
  package directions
2 tbsp margarine
⅓ cup grated Parmesan cheese
2 eggs, beaten
1 pound ground beef
½ cup chopped onion
¼ cup chopped green pepper
1 (16 oz) can tomatoes, crushed or
  finely chopped, with liquid
1 (6 oz) can tomato paste
1 tsp sugar
1 tsp dried oregano
¼ tsp salt
¼ tsp garlic salt
2 cups cottage cheese, or more to
  taste
1½ cups grated mozzarella cheese,
  or more to taste

Jo Ann likes dishes that can be prepared in advance, "We always cook plenty," she says. "I like an abundance of food."

1. To cooked spaghetti, add margarine, Parmesan and eggs. Coat 2 (9-inch) pie pans with nonstick cooking spray. Put half spaghetti mixture in each pan, arranging it across the bottom and around the edges to form crusts.

2. In skillet cook meat and drain fat; add onion and green pepper. Cook until vegetables are tender, 5 to 10 minutes. Add tomatoes, tomato paste, sugar, oregano, salt and garlic salt; blend.

3. Top each spaghetti crust with ½ the cottage cheese, then ½ the beef mixture. Allow about ½ inch of spaghetti "crust" to show around top edge. Cover pans loosely with foil.

4. Bake at 350 degrees about 1 hour. Uncover. Sprinkle half the mozzarella cheese on each pie. Bake 5 minutes more. Cool 5 to 10 minutes. Slice into wedges and serve.

Note: Pies may be frozen after Step 3. When ready to serve, thaw and cook as directed in Step 4.

Makes 2 (9-inch) pies, about 6 servings each

Cavatini

Melinda McKinzie, Kansas City, Missouri

Melinda saves time (and cuts fat) by cooking her beef in a microwave oven. The beef is put in a microwave-safe dish with a lid and a drain insert. Melinda then cooks the beef 2 to 3 minutes, stirs and cooks 2 to 3 minutes more. The cooked beef is drained and ready for casseroles.

1. Cook pasta according to package directions; drain well and set aside.

2. Brown ground beef in skillet over medium-high heat with onions and green pepper until onion is translucent, about 5 to 8 minutes, or cook in microwave.

3. Stir in pepperoni, and cook until heated through. Drain fat from pan. Combine sauce and meat mixture; simmer 5 minutes.

4. Arrange half the pasta in lightly greased 3-quart casserole. Spoon on half the meat mixture, spread with cottage cheese and sprinkle with half the mozzarella.

5. Arrange remaining half pasta on top, spoon on remaining meat mixture and top with remaining mozzarella.

6. Bake, uncovered, in at 350 degrees 30 to 35 minutes, or until heated through.

Note: This dish can be prepared for later baking.

Makes 8 servings

3 cups mixed, uncooked pasta, such as 1 cup each rigatoni and mostaccioli plus ½ cup each rotini and shell macaroni
1 pound ground beef
½ medium onion, chopped
½ green pepper, chopped
3 ounces pepperoni, sliced
1 (28 to 30 oz) jar spaghetti sauce
1 cup cream-style cottage cheese
12 ounces mozzarella, grated

Poultry

Chicken Potato Pie

Vikki Mitcheltree, Independence, Missouri

1 (9-inch) deep-dish pie shell, baked
2 tbsp cooking oil, such as canola
2 boneless, skinless chicken breasts
  cut into bite-size pieces
¼ cup chopped celery
¼ cup chopped onion
¼ cup chopped pimento, or chopped
  red bell pepper
¼ cup chopped mushrooms
2 cups frozen mixed vegetables (corn,
  carrots, peas, green beans)
1½ cups chicken broth
8 ounces cream cheese, cut into
  small pieces
½ tsp dry tarragon
½ tsp dry dill
½ tsp seasoned salt
½ tsp garlic powder
¼ tsp ground black pepper
1 tbsp cornstarch
¼ cup water
4 cups mashed potatoes (see note)
¼ cup grated Parmesan cheese
1 tsp paprika

"I like to have things in the freezer that I can come home and put in the oven and have it ready," Vikki says.

1. Heat oil in large skillet over medium heat. Add chicken; cook and stir until cooked through.

2. Add celery, onion, pimento and mushrooms. Cook and stir until tender. Add mixed vegetables and heat until thawed and tender. Set aside.

3. Pour chicken broth into large saucepan. Add cream cheese, tarragon, dill, seasoned salt, garlic powder and black pepper. Cook and stir over medium heat until smooth.

4. Dissolve cornstarch in water; add to cheese mixture. Cook and stir until thick. Reduce heat to low; add chicken-and-vegetable mixture. Stir until well-mixed. Pour into baked pie shell. Top with mashed potatoes. Sprinkle with Parmesan cheese and paprika.

5. Bake at 350 degrees 60 minutes, or until golden brown and bubbly.

Note: Six medium potatoes will make about 4 cups mashed potatoes.

Makes 6 to 8 servings

Chicken by Candlelight

Janice Walton, Kansas City, Missouri

Elegant but quick. That's the way Janice likes all her dishes.

1. In a bowl, mix together all ingredients except chicken.

2. Place chicken breasts, skin-side down, in a glass baking dish large enough to hold chicken without crowding. Pour mixture over chicken.

3. Bake uncovered at 325 degrees 1½ hours; turn chicken skin-side up, and bake 30 more minutes. Chicken will be nicely browned.

Makes 6 servings

1 cup dry white wine
1 tbsp lemon juice
½ tsp paprika
½ tsp black pepper
½ cup (1 stick) melted butter
¼ cup chopped green onions
¼ cup minced parsley
¼ cup orange juice
1 tsp salt
6 chicken breast halves

Good Neighbor Chicken

Pamela Comninellis, Kansas City, Missouri

Pamela looks for recipes that are simple but "have a pretty gourmet presentation."

1. Cut dried beef or ham in strips and scatter on bottom of greased 9- by 13-inch baking dish.

2. Wrap a bacon strip around each piece of chicken, and place on top of meat.

3. Mix soup, sherry and curry, and pour over chicken. Bake uncovered at 300 degrees 2½ to 3 hours, or until golden brown on top and sauce is slightly thickened. Serve over rice. Peas and fruit salad go well with this dish.

Makes 8 servings

½ pound dried beef or ham, or a
   mixture of both
8 slices bacon
8 boneless chicken breast halves
2 (10.5 oz) cans cream of chicken
   soup
1 cup sherry
2 tbsp curry powder, or to taste

20-Minute Chicken Creole

Cynthia Davis, Kansas City, Missouri

4 medium chicken breast halves (1½
    pounds total), skinned, boned and
    cut into 1-inch strips, or
    substitute 1 pound already
    skinned and boned breasts
1 (15 oz) can tomatoes, cut up, with
    liquid
1 cup low-sodium chili sauce
1½ cups chopped green pepper (1
    large pepper)
½ cup chopped celery
¼ cup chopped onion
2 cloves garlic, minced
1 tbsp chopped fresh basil, or 1 tsp
    crushed dried basil
1 tbsp chopped fresh parsley, or 1 tsp
    dried parsley
¼ tsp crushed red pepper
¼ tsp salt
Hot cooked rice, or whole wheat
    pasta

This simple low-fat recipe is one Cynthia, a registered dietitian, uses when teaching people how to cut their fat intake.

1. Spray deep skillet with nonstick cooking spray. Preheat pan over high heat until hot but not smoking. Add chicken strips to hot skillet; cook, stirring, 3 to 5 minutes, or until no longer pink.

2. Reduce heat. Add remaining ingredients except rice. Bring to a boil; reduce heat and simmer, covered, 10 minutes, until vegetables are tender but not soft.

3. Serve over hot cooked rice or whole wheat pasta.

Adapted from *Down Home Healthy Cooking* (The National Cancer Institute of the National Institutes of Health).

Makes 4 servings

Chicken Cacciatore

Daisy Mason Hanson, Kansas City, Missouri

Daisy, who has diabetes, relies on recipes such as this one based on a dish from *The Art of Cooking for the Diabetic* by Katharine Middleton and Mary Abbott Hess.

1. Preheat oven to 400 degrees. Prepare a large casserole by coating with nonstick cooking spray.

2. Wipe chicken pieces with damp cloth. Heat vegetable oil in large frying pan. Brown chicken on both sides. Transfer chicken to casserole.

3. Cook onions and pepper strips in frying pan 3 to 4 minutes, stirring frequently.

4. In a bowl, combine tomatoes with remaining ingredients; mix well. Add to onions and green pepper strips. Bring to a boil and pour evenly over the top of the chicken.

5. Bake 30 minutes. Turn chicken and baste with the sauce; bake an additional 20 to 30 minutes, or until chicken is tender.

Makes 4 servings

1 chicken (2½ pounds), cut in pieces
1 tbsp vegetable oil
½ cup chopped onions
½ cup finely cut strips of green pepper
1 (16 oz) can tomatoes, cut up, with liquid
⅓ cup tomato paste
¾ tsp salt

⅛ tsp garlic powder, optional
½ tsp oregano
¼ cup lemon juice
½ cup water

Chicken Mosca

Martha Hiatt, Prairie Village, Kansas

2 small chickens, about 2 pounds
    each, or 6 chicken breast halves
Salt and freshly ground black pepper,
    to taste
1 cup (2 sticks) butter, divided
10 cloves garlic, minced
½ cup fresh parsley, minced
⅛ cup fresh basil, minced, optional

Martha grew up in southern Louisiana, and her grandparents are from Lebanon. "You take the heritage of my family and the environment where I lived, and that's the cooking that I do," she says.

1. Cut chicken into serving-size pieces. Remove skin. Season chicken with salt and black pepper.

2. Melt 1 stick butter in a heavy pot or heavy Dutch oven over medium heat. When butter has melted, add chicken parts and fry until lightly golden on outside, 5 to 10 minutes. Work in batches if necessary, and add more butter if necessary to keep chicken from sticking.

3. In a small pot, melt remaining stick of butter and add garlic; let simmer about 1 minute. Pour the butter mixture over chicken in the pot; turn chicken over several times until butter mixture coats all chicken pieces. Reduce heat to low; cover and cook about 1 hour, or until chicken is fork-tender.

4. Add parsley and optional basil; turn chicken to coat with herbs. Serve with white rice or favorite pasta and hot French bread.

Variation: Substitute thyme or rosemary for basil.

Makes 6 servings

Grilled Spicy Chicken with Two Sauces

Susan Hill, Kansas City, Missouri

1. Mix together brown sugar, sage, cumin, thyme, salt and cayenne; rub over chicken pieces. Place chicken on broiler pan and bake at 350 degrees 40 minutes.

2. Remove from oven and place chicken on grill over hot coals, turning once, until browned and crisp, about 5 to 10 minutes total. Serve hot with Peanut Sauce and Fruit Salsa.

Makes 6 servings

3 tbsp brown sugar
2 tsp sage
2 tsp ground cumin
2 tsp thyme
1 tsp salt
½ tsp cayenne pepper
6 combination leg-thigh pieces
   chicken
Peanut sauce (recipe follows)
Fruit salsa (recipe follows)

Peanut Sauce

Susan Hill, Kansas City, Missouri

1. Cook olive oil and shallots 5 minutes over moderate heat. Whisk in the peanut butter, coconut milk, lemon juice and soy sauce.

2. Stir in water and cook, stirring often, 5 minutes. Stir in brown sugar and chili paste. Cook 5 minutes.

3. Remove from heat and stir in basil. Serve warm.

Makes 2 to 2½ cups

2 tsp olive oil
4 tsp minced shallots
¾ cup chunky natural peanut butter
6 tbsp unsweetened coconut milk
¼ cup fresh lemon juice
¼ cup soy sauce
¾ cup water
2 tbsp brown sugar, packed
1 tsp Asian chili paste
¼ cup chopped basil

Fruit Salsa

Susan Hill, Kansas City, Missouri

2 cups diced fresh pineapple
1 cup diced cantaloupe
½ large sweet onion, diced
2 medium tomatoes, diced
1 jalapeno pepper, minced
¼ cup to ½ cup chopped fresh
   cilantro, to taste
¾ tsp to 1 tsp ground cumin, to taste
1 tsp minced garlic
½ tsp salt

1. Combine all ingredients, cover and refrigerate at least 1 hour before serving. This salsa is also great just served with tortilla chips.

Makes about 5 cups

Chicken-Noodle Stir-Fry

Brenda Lang, Blue Springs, Missouri

4 cups fine egg noodles
2 medium chicken breast halves
2 tbsp oil
1 small onion, chopped
1 tbsp minced garlic
1 medium carrot, shredded
3 tbsp soy sauce
1 (8 oz) can water chestnuts
Garlic salt and black pepper to taste
½ cup chicken broth

1. Cook noodles as directed; drain and set aside.

2. Simmer chicken breasts, covered, in large pot of salted water 20 minutes, or until cooked through and meat pulls easily from bone. Set cooked chicken aside until cool enough to handle, then remove meat from skin and bones. Chop chicken into bite-size pieces.

3. In a wok or large skillet, heat oil over medium heat. Add onion and garlic, and sauté 5 minutes, or until translucent. Add carrots, soy sauce, water chestnuts, garlic salt, black pepper and chopped chicken. Mix until well blended. Add cooked noodles and chicken broth, and heat through. Serve hot.

Makes 10 servings

Arroz con Pollo

Nanci Hirschorn, Overland Park, Kansas

Nanci enjoys a variety of tastes, and calls her version of Arroz con Pollo a "poor man's paella."

1. For marinade: Combine all marinade ingredients, except chicken. Coat chicken with mixture, cover and marinate 1 hour in refrigerator.

2. For rice and chicken pot: Heat 3 tablespoons olive oil in 5-quart flameproof casserole or Dutch oven over medium heat; add garlic and onion. Sauté until tender, 3 to 5 minutes.

3. Add chicken stock and beer, saffron (crumble while adding), paprika and rice. Bring to a boil. Reduce heat to low, and simmer 20 to 25 minutes, or until rice is tender and liquid is absorbed.

4. Meanwhile, place chicken and marinade in large skillet over medium-high heat. Sauté until almost done, about 5 to 10 minutes. Cut into bite-size pieces and set aside.

5. About 5 minutes before rice is done, add to pot the cooked chicken, red peppers, artichoke hearts, olives and peas; stir and cook 5 minutes.

6. Just before serving, stir in capers.

Makes 6 servings

For marinade:
4 cloves garlic, minced
1 tsp oregano
1 tsp thyme
2 tbsp olive oil
Juice of 1 lemon
Ground black pepper, to taste
6 boneless chicken breast halves

For rice and chicken pot:
3 tbsp olive oil
3 cloves garlic, minced
1 onion, chopped
2 cups chicken stock
2 cups beer
½ tsp saffron
1 tsp paprika
2 cups uncooked rice
2 red bell peppers, cut into large dice
1 (14 oz) can artichoke hearts, quartered and drained
1 (4.25 oz) can chopped black olives, drained
1 (10 oz) box frozen peas, thawed
1 (3 oz) bottle capers, drained

Chicken Piccata

Judy Hughes, Kansas City, Missouri

6 lemons
5 to 6 skinless boneless chicken
   breasts (2 to 3 pounds) (cut each
   breast in half)
All-purpose flour
2 tsp white pepper, or to taste
½ cup (1 stick) butter or margarine,
   or mixture of ¼ cup (½ stick)
   butter and ¼ cup olive oil
½ cup white wine, or water

Judy's extensive travels, which included living in Italy for a time, allowed her to learn many cooking styles: "I learned by watching and trying," she says, "and by having a hunger for [learning]."

1. Juice 4 lemons and slice remaining 2 lemons.

2. Pound chicken with edge of saucer until thin (about ¼ inch).

3. Dip each chicken piece into lemon juice, then dredge lightly with flour. Reserve remaining lemon juice. Lay prepared chicken on waxed paper until all are coated, then sprinkle all pieces equally with white pepper.

3. Heat butter in skillet over medium heat until hot, but not smoking. Sauté chicken pieces until golden brown, 2 to 3 minutes on each side. Work in batches so chicken will not be crowded.

4. Bake at 200 degrees 20 minutes.

5. Meanwhile, brown lemon slices in pan drippings; remove slices and set aside.

6. Pour remainder of lemon juice and wine into hot pan drippings. Bring to a boil and reduce over medium heat while scraping bits from bottom of pan.

7. When ready to serve, pour mixture over chicken, and top each piece with browned lemon slice.

Variation: Substitute 2 pounds thinly sliced veal for chicken.

Makes 6 to 8 servings

Chicken Wellington

Beth Markley, Merriam, Kansas

Beth's husband limits his fat intake, but she shares her richer recipes, such as Chicken Wellington, with friends.

1. Thaw pastry 20 minutes.

2. Sprinkle chicken with thyme, salt and black pepper. Heat 3 tablespoons margarine in skillet over medium-high heat; add chicken, and brown. Remove chicken from pan and set aside.

3. Add remaining 2 tablespoons margarine to skillet and reduce heat to medium. Add onion and mushrooms; cook until tender, about 5 minutes. Stir in parsley.

4. On a lightly floured surface, roll each pastry sheet to a 14-inch square. Cut each sheet into 4 (7-inch) squares.

5. In a small bowl, combine cream cheese with mustard; spread over one side of each chicken half. Spread each pastry square with 2 tablespoons mushroom mixture; top with chicken breast.

6. Brush edges of pastry with water; bring corners of pastry to center and press edges together to seal. Place seam side down about 1½ inches apart on ungreased baking sheets. Brush tops with egg white–water mixture.

7. Bake at 375 degrees 25 minutes, or until puffed and golden brown.

Makes 8 servings

1 (17 oz) package frozen puff pastry sheets
8 boneless chicken breast halves
2 tsp dried thyme leaves
Salt and freshly ground black pepper, to taste
5 tbsp margarine, divided
1 onion, finely chopped
¼ pound fresh mushrooms, sliced
2 tbsp chopped parsley
3 ounces cream cheese, at room temperature
2 tbsp Dijon-style mustard
1 egg white whisked together with 2 tbsp water

Chicken Breast with Cranberry-Orange Sauce

Dennis McWilliams, Kansas City, Kansas

2 large onions, sliced ½-inch thick
6 boneless, skinless chicken breast
    halves
¼ cup frozen orange juice
    concentrate, thawed but not
    diluted
¼ cup water

For cranberry-orange sauce:
1 (16 oz) can whole-berry cranberry
    sauce
1 tsp grated orange rind
¾ cup unsweetened orange juice

2 tbsp brown sugar
2 tsp cornstarch
Orange slices, for garnish

Health concerns now dictate that Dennis avoid fat and cholesterol. Those rigors haven't hurt his cooking style; they've just changed it. "It didn't make a difference like I thought it would," he says.

1. Place onion slices in bottom of ungreased 9- by 13- by 2-inch baking dish. Top with chicken.

2. Mix orange juice concentrate and water in bowl. Baste breasts with orange juice mixture. Bake 1 hour at 350 degrees, until cooked through and browned. Baste occasionally with orange juice mixture.

3. Meanwhile, make cranberry-orange sauce: Combine all sauce ingredients in small saucepan; stir well. Bring to a boil over high heat, stirring constantly. Reduce heat to medium, and cook 1 minute, stirring until thickened. Serve warm.

4. When chicken is done, transfer to serving plates. Discard onions. Spoon cranberry-orange sauce over chicken. Garnish with orange slices and serve.

Makes 6 servings

Chicken Tetrazzini

Doris Quinn, Independence, Missouri

Former Missouri state legislator Doris Quinn included this recipe in a cookbook she wrote for husbands.

1. Place water in large pan, add salt and bring to a boil over high heat. Break spaghetti into 3-inch pieces and add to boiling water. Cook until spaghetti is tender, about 8 minutes.

2. Meanwhile, melt margarine in a large saucepan over low-medium heat, add flour and mix thoroughly. Gradually stir in chicken stock, chicken pieces, pimento and olives; cook until slightly thickened, 5 to 10 minutes.

3. When the spaghetti is cooked, drain and divide between 2 (2-quart) casseroles, distributing spaghetti evenly over the bottom. Top spaghetti in each dish with half the chicken mixture.

4. Cube the cheddar and provolone cheese; top each casserole with half the cheese mixture. Freeze one dish for later. Bake other dish at 350 degrees 45 minutes, or until heated through and cheese is melted. To bake after freezing, thaw and bake as usual, or heat in microwave.

Makes 2 (4-serving) casseroles

3 quarts water
1 tbsp salt
8 ounces thin spaghetti
1 cup (2 sticks) margarine
1 cup all-purpose flour
1 quart chicken stock
1 pound cooked, boned chicken
2 ounces chopped pimento, with
   liquid
4 ounces sliced black olives, drained
2 ounces cheddar cheese
2 ounces provolone or Romano
   cheese

Chicken Pasta Delight

Joanne Smith, Kansas City, Missouri

1 tbsp olive oil
2 tbsp butter
2 whole chicken breasts, cut into
   finger-size strips
⅛ tsp seasoned salt
⅛ tsp coarsely ground black pepper
¼ tsp oregano
¼ tsp basil
¼ tsp Italian seasoning
15 cloves garlic, 5 crushed and 10
   sautéed until soft in 1 tbsp olive oil
1 tbsp capers
8 ounces spaghetti, cooked according
   to package directions
Freshly grated Parmesan cheese

1. Heat olive oil and butter over medium-high heat. Add chicken strips, and sauté until cooked through.

2. Add remaining ingredients, except spaghetti and Parmesan cheese. Add cooked spaghetti; toss.

3. Serve immediately. Top with Parmesan cheese.

Variations: Substitute ½ pound medium shrimp (peeled and deveined), or ½-pound salmon fillet for chicken.

Makes 6 servings

Savory Yogurt Chicken

Karen Snedden, Lee's Summit, Missouri

Karen describes this dish as "unusual and really good."

1. In a pie plate, stir together bread crumbs, Parmesan cheese, onion, garlic powder, seasoned salt, oregano, thyme and black pepper. Rinse chicken; pat dry. Coat chicken with yogurt; roll in crumb mixture.

2. Place chicken, meaty side up, in a lightly greased 15- by 10- by 1-inch baking dish or pan. Drizzle melted margarine over top. Sprinkle with sesame seeds.

3. Bake, uncovered, at 375 degrees 45 to 55 minutes, or till tender. Serve with Creamy Yogurt Sauce.

Makes 8 servings

1 cup fine dry bread crumbs
¼ cup grated Parmesan cheese
2 tbsp dried minced onion, or to taste
1 tsp garlic powder
1 tsp seasoned salt
¼ tsp dried oregano, crushed
¼ tsp dried thyme, crushed
½ tsp ground black pepper
4 whole medium chicken breasts, skinned and cut in half
8 ounces plain yogurt
¼ cup (½ stick) margarine or butter, melted
2 tsp sesame seeds
Creamy Yogurt Sauce (recipe follows)

Creamy Yogurt Sauce

Karen Snedden, Lee's Summit, Missouri

1. In medium saucepan, combine all ingredients. Cook over low heat, stirring occasionally, until heated through.

Makes about 2½ cups

1 (10.5 oz) can cream of chicken soup
8 ounces plain yogurt
½ cup chicken broth
1 tsp lemon juice
½ tsp Worcestershire sauce
½ tsp garlic powder, or to taste
½ tsp seasoned salt, or to taste

Rock Cornish Hens

Tish Tucker, Kansas City, Missouri

2 Rock Cornish hens
1 (6 oz) box long-grain and wild rice
¼ cup slivered almonds
1 tbsp margarine, melted
½ cup white wine

This recipe has special meaning for Tish and her husband Jim. It was the dish that cemented their romance when they were dating years ago.

1. Thaw hens, and remove giblets. Rinse in cold water, pat dry with paper towels, wiping cavity well.

2. Prepare rice according to package directions. Add slivered almonds. (May be prepared the night before or several hours in advance up to this point.)

3. Just before roasting, stuff birds, filling loosely; close cavity with poultry pins. Brush hens with melted margarine, and place in roasting pan.

4. Bake at 325 degrees 1½ hours, or until golden brown. Legs should be loose in the joints. During last half-hour of baking, baste hens with white wine.

5. Split hens in half and serve, or leave whole for 2 generous servings. Goes well with fresh asparagus or broccoli with hollandaise sauce.

Makes 2 to 4 servings

Quail Baked in Mushroom Wine Sauce

Jean Rose, Overland Park, Kansas

Jean appreciates this quail recipe for the flexibility of the baking time.

1. Rinse and dry quail. Season with salt and black pepper, then coat with flour. Melt butter in large skillet over medium heat. Working in batches, sauté quail on both sides until brown, about 10 minutes. Arrange in ovenproof casserole large enough to comfortably accommodate the quail in one layer (about 2 quarts).

2. In the large skillet, sauté green onions and mushrooms until lightly browned, 7 to 10 minutes. (If necessary, add more butter to skillet to keep vegetables from sticking.)

3. Add cream of mushroom soup, sour cream and white wine; blend well. Stir in parsley, thyme, salt and black pepper, to taste. Pour over quail.

4. Bake, covered with foil, in preheated oven at 350 degrees about 45 minutes. Uncover and bake 15 minutes more, or until golden and tender.

Note: Dish can hold in oven several minutes before serving. Serve over wild rice.

Variation: Substitute 6 chicken breast halves for quail.

Makes 6 servings

12 quail, dressed and split
Salt and ground black pepper, to taste
All-purpose flour, for dredging
3 tbsp butter
4 to 6 green onions, chopped
½ pound fresh mushrooms, chopped
1 (10.5 oz) can cream of mushroom soup
1 cup sour cream
1 (10.5 oz) soup can of dry white wine
½ cup chopped fresh parsley
1 tbsp dry thyme leaves

Seafood

Shrimp Curry
Anne Bennett, Mission Hills, Kansas

1 onion, chopped
1 clove garlic, minced
4 tbsp butter
3 tbsp all-purpose flour
2 tbsp curry powder
1 cup chicken stock
1 cup half-and-half, or milk
1 pound large shrimp, shelled and
    deveined
Salt to taste
Cooked rice

For condiments:
Chopped peanuts
Grated hard-cooked eggs
Chopped green onions
Chutney

You can use leftover turkey in place of the shrimp for a tasty and simple dish.

1. Sauté onion and garlic in butter until soft.

2. Sprinkle with flour and curry powder. Cook 3 minutes over medium heat, or until well-combined and bubbly. Gradually add chicken stock and half-and-half, stirring constantly.

3. Add shrimp and simmer until shrimp are cooked, about 5 minutes.

4. Add salt to taste, and serve over cooked rice with the peanuts, eggs, green onions and chutney as condiments.

Variation: In place of shrimp, use cooked skinned, boned, sliced chicken breast, or leftover turkey, cut into bite-size chunks.

Makes 4 servings

Crab Corn Muffins

Evie Bresette, Kansas City, Missouri

"If I see a recipe, I think, 'How can I make it low-fat? What can I do to substitute this or that?' " Evie says. Here is one result.

1. Chop crabmeat into bite-size pieces and combine with onion and green pepper.

2. In a large bowl mix the creamed corn, egg, cornmeal and skim milk. Add crab mixture, cheese, salt, baking powder, garlic powder, tarragon, rosemary, thyme and Tabasco.

3. Spray large (4-inch) muffin tins with nonstick cooking spray, and fill ⅔ full.

4. Bake at 400 degrees 30 minutes, or until toothpick inserted in center comes out clean, and tops are golden brown.

5. Let sit 10 minutes before lifting out of tins. Place muffins on plate and top with about 2 tablespoons seafood sauce.

Makes 5 servings

8 ounces mock crabmeat
½ cup chopped onion
½ cup chopped green pepper
1 (15 oz) can creamed corn
1 egg
1½ cups cornmeal
½ cup skim milk
1 (6 oz) package grated low-fat
    cheddar cheese
½ tsp salt
1 tbsp baking powder
1 tsp garlic powder
¼ tsp dried tarragon
¼ tsp ground rosemary
½ tsp thyme
¼ tsp Tabasco sauce, or to taste
Seafood cocktail sauce

Louisiana Rice

Anna Hicks, Kansas City, Missouri

2½ cups uncooked rice
½ cup vegetable oil
4 cups chicken broth
1½ tsp dry oregano
1 tsp seasoned salt, such as Lawry's
Ground black pepper, to taste
1½ pounds shrimp, peeled and
    deveined
1 cup frozen corn
1 cup frozen peas
1 large onion, chopped
1 large bell pepper, chopped
1½ cups chopped celery
½ pound fresh mushrooms, sliced
1 large clove garlic, minced

1. Place rice and oil in large pan over low heat, and brown the rice.

2. Add chicken broth, oregano, seasoned salt, black pepper and shrimp. Bring to a boil over high heat, reduce to low, cover and simmer about 10 minutes.

3. Add corn, peas, onion, bell pepper, celery, mushrooms and garlic, and mix well. Cover and cook until rice is tender and liquid is absorbed, about 10 minutes more.

4. Serve hot.

Variation: Substitute 1½ pounds cooked chicken, or a combination of chicken and shrimp, for the 1½ pounds shrimp.

Makes 10 servings

Grilled Basil Shrimp

Greg Lear, Kansas City, Missouri

1. Combine wine, olive oil, lemon juice, mustard, chopped basil and peppercorns. Pour over shrimp in shallow bowl. Marinate in refrigerator at least 3 hours, turning shrimp occasionally.

2. Prepare coals for grilling. Remove shrimp from marinade, reserving marinade. Wrap the middle of each shrimp with a basil leaf, then with a slice of prosciutto.

3. Thread four shrimp lengthwise, starting at the head, on each of 6 metal skewers. Try to place shrimp at a slight angle to catch prosciutto with skewer.

4. Bring reserved marinade to a boil, and boil 2 minutes.

5. Grill shrimp about 6 inches from hot coals, basting with reserved marinade, 4 to 5 minutes on each side, or until shrimp are opaque. If using kettle-style grill, cover with vented lid while cooking.

Adapted from *The Silver Palate Good Times Cookbook.*

Makes 6 servings as a main course, 24 as an appetizer

1 cup dry white wine
1 cup olive oil
¼ cup fresh lemon juice
2 tbsp Dijon-style mustard
½ cup chopped fresh basil
Freshly cracked black peppercorns
24 jumbo shrimp, peeled and deveined, with tails left on
24 whole large basil leaves
24 thin slices prosciutto, trimmed of fat

Scallop-Vegetable Vermicelli

Marcy VanLandingham, Shawnee, Kansas

2 cloves garlic, minced
1 cup julienned carrots
2 cups diagonally sliced celery
2 tbsp olive oil
1½ cups peeled and chopped
    tomatoes
½ cup sliced green onions
1 cup sliced fresh mushrooms
1½ pounds scallops
2 tsp grated fresh ginger root
¼ tsp salt
¼ tsp white pepper
½ cup Sauterne wine
3 cups hot cooked vermicelli, cooked
    without salt or fat

"I really love to eat, but I don't want to get fat," Marcy says. "I feel better (eating low-fat foods), and I am going to be able to eat what I want more if I keep healthy food around the house."

1. Sauté garlic, carrots and celery in olive oil in a skillet over medium heat 5 minutes, or until slightly tender, stirring often.

2. Add tomatoes, green onions, mushrooms, scallops, ginger root, salt and white pepper; cook 5 minutes, stirring often, until scallops are firm and opaque.

3. Add wine, and cook an additional 3 minutes until heated through. (Don't overcook, or scallops will be tough.)

4. Serve over hot cooked vermicelli.

Makes 4 to 6 servings

Shrimp a la Jim

The Watson Family, Johnson County, Kansas

This recipe is named in honor of Irene Watson's late husband Jim. Each week, Irene and her children—Dee Dee, Jim II and Kathy—gather to cook and commune. This recipe is a family favorite and a lovely reminder of Jim.

1. Fry bacon in large pan over medium heat until crisp. Drain bacon on paper towels, and pour grease from pan.

2. Return bacon to pan and return pan to heat; add onions, green pepper and celery. Cover and simmer on low heat until soft, about 20 minutes; stir occasionally.

3. Add remaining ingredients, except shrimp and rice. Stir to combine, and simmer 15 minutes.

4. Add shrimp and heat through. Serve at once over hot steamed rice.

Makes 6 to 8 servings

3 slices bacon, diced
2 medium onions, diced
1 medium green pepper, diced
5 ribs celery, diced
1 (15 oz) can tomatoes
1 (10 oz) can tomato and green chilies
1 (10 oz) package frozen chopped okra
1 tsp dried thyme leaves
1 tsp cayenne
1 tsp salt
½ tsp ground black pepper
1 bay leaf
½ cup chili sauce
2 pounds shrimp, cooked and shelled
8 cups hot cooked rice

Seafood Pasta Sauce

Janet Butcher, Lenexa, Kansas

1 green bell pepper, cut into 1-inch
  dice
4 ounces sliced fresh mushrooms
1 tsp canola, or other light oil
2 (15 oz) cans Italian-style tomato
  sauce
2 (15 oz) cans Italian-style stewed
  tomatoes, cut up, with liquid
1 (6 oz) can tomato paste
½ pound medium shrimp, cooked
  and shelled
1 (10 oz) can whole baby clams,
  drained
Hot cooked rotini or tubular pasta,
  about 1½ pounds uncooked
  weight

"I like doing a lot of different things, and I like to experiment," Janet says. That's how she created this seafood pasta sauce.

1. Sauté green pepper and mushrooms in oil over medium heat 5 minutes, or until just tender. Remove with slotted spoon and set aside.

2. In large pot, combine tomato sauce, tomatoes and tomato paste. Heat to boiling. Add shrimp and clams. Reduce heat to low, cover and simmer 15 minutes.

3. Add green peppers and mushrooms. Cook 5 more minutes, covered, until heated through. Serve over hot cooked pasta.

Makes 8 to 10 servings

Linguine with Crabmeat and Mushrooms

Henry Teri, Lee's Summit, Missouri

Henry and his wife, Bev, lead a hurried life, like many of us. Henry and Bev find that simple pasta dishes are often the best and tastiest solution for dinner.

1. Sauté garlic in 1 tablespoon of olive oil over low to medium heat; do not let garlic brown.

2. Add remaining olive oil, mushrooms and shallots, and sauté 2 to 3 minutes to soften.

3. Add lemon juice, black pepper and crabmeat blend, and cook 2 to 3 minutes, stirring occasionally to heat through. Pour over hot cooked linguine and serve.

Makes 4 servings

6 cloves garlic, minced
⅓ cup olive oil, divided
1 pound fresh button mushrooms, sliced
2 shallots, chopped
2 tbsp lemon juice
¼ tsp freshly ground black pepper
1 pound crabmeat blend
1 pound linguine, cooked and hot

Melt-in-Your-Mouth Salmon

Nate Kubel, Overland Park, Kansas

¼ cup (½ stick) unsalted butter
3 tbsp Dijon country-style mustard
3 tbsp brown sugar
Juice of ½ lime
2 pounds salmon fillet

1. In small saucepan, melt butter. Stir in mustard and brown sugar until sugar is dissolved. Squeeze in the juice. Remove from heat.

2. Brush sauce on flesh side of salmon. Place in lightly greased fish basket; cook, skin-side down, on barbecue grill about 3 inches above coals at medium-high heat 8 to 10 minutes, until top begins to lose its glossy appearance and the fish flesh begins to get firm.

3. Turn, and cook 2 minutes more, or until firm to touch.

4. Pour any remaining sauce on salmon before serving. Serve with boiled potatoes tossed with butter and dill.

Note: If any salmon is left over, serve cold with melted sauce as an appetizer or main course.

Makes 4 servings

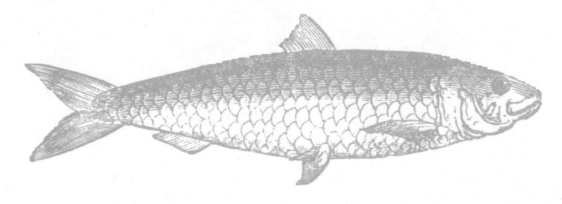

Pacific Cod Parmesan

David and JoAnn Lesh, Prairie Village, Kansas

David and JoAnn split their time between Prairie Village and Glacier Bay, Alaska. Most cod is fresh-frozen on commercial fishing boats. If properly thawed (gradually, in the refrigerator), David and JoAnn say Alaskan cod will taste nearly as good as fresh.

1. Cut fillets into serving-size pieces. Mix together flour, salt and black pepper in shallow bowl or pie plate. Beat eggs in a separate shallow bowl. Combine bread crumbs and Parmesan cheese in another shallow bowl or pie plate.

2. One at a time, roll fish in flour mixture to coat, dip in beaten eggs, then coat with crumb mixture. Place on lightly greased cookie sheet.

3. Bake at 400 degrees 10 to 15 minutes. Fish is done when an instant-reading thermometer registers 140 degrees when placed in thickest part of fish.

4. Place fish on platter with lemon wedges. Serve with tartar sauce or seafood cocktail sauce with horseradish.

Makes 4 to 6 servings

2 pounds Pacific cod fillets
About 1 cup all-purpose flour
1/2 tsp salt
1/2 tsp ground black pepper
3 eggs
1 cup grated sourdough bread
    crumbs
1/4 cup grated fresh Parmesan cheese
Lemon wedges

Vatapa

Doug Auwarter, Kansas City, Missouri

4 tbsp olive oil, divided
1 pound boneless chicken breast, cut
  into 1-inch dice
1 onion, chopped
1 tomato, chopped
1 Anaheim chili, finely chopped
2 to 3 cloves garlic, minced
1 cube fish bouillon, such as Knorr,
  dissolved in 2 cups water
1 (14 oz) can unsweetened coconut
  milk
2 tbsp creamy-style peanut butter
½ tsp sesame oil
1 tsp paprika
1 pound cod, or other firm white fish,
  cut into 1-inch dice
1 pound medium shrimp, peeled and
  deveined
About ½ cup bread crumbs

Doug described himself as a "full-fledged Brazil nut." He fell in love with Brazilian music and immersed himself in the culture, including cooking. In Brazil cooks grate a fresh coconut and boil the meat in its milk with water, ground dried shrimp and ground peanuts. That mixture is then strained. This vatapa recipe, while easier, retains the flavor and texture of the Brazilian dish.

1. In a 12-inch skillet over high heat, heat 2 tablespoons olive oil. Add chicken, and sauté until lightly browned.

2. Add onion, tomato, chili and garlic; reduce heat to medium and sauté until softened, 6 to 8 minutes.

3. Add fish stock and deglaze pan. When mixture comes to a boil, add coconut milk and peanut butter, bring to a boil. Simmer until reduced by ½ cup, about 10 minutes.

4. While mixture is simmering, heat remaining 2 tablespoons olive oil and sesame oil in a small pan over medium heat; add paprika. Remove from heat.

5. When mixture in large skillet is reduced, add fish pieces, shrimp and paprika-oil mixture; mix well. Add bread crumbs, a little at a time, until the consistency of a thick gravy is reached. Serve over white rice.

Notes: Unsweetened coconut milk is available at Asian markets. The paprika-sesame oil substitutes for red palm oil. As a time-saver, chop onion, tomatoes, chili and garlic together in food processor before sautéing.

Makes 6 to 8 servings

Mackerel Croquettes

Catherine May, Kansas City, Missouri

Mackerel croquettes are an economical alternative to salmon croquettes, and the dish was popular among Catherine's clients during her career as a home economist for local extension offices.

1. In a bowl, mix together all ingredients, except corn oil. Blend well.

2. Form into croquettes.

3. Heat corn oil in large heavy skillet over medium heat until hot. Add croquettes, and fry until nicely browned on one side, about 10 minutes. Turn, and brown on other side, cooking about 10 minutes more.

4. Serve hot or cold. Leftovers are good in sandwiches.

Makes 6 to 7 croquettes

1 (15 oz) can mackerel, including liquid
1 egg
½ cup cornmeal
¼ cup all-purpose flour
¼ cup chopped onions
¼ chopped green pepper
¼ cup corn oil

Marinated and Grilled Salmon

Marsha Schweiger, Overland Park, Kansas

1 cup dry white wine
¼ cup lemon juice
2 tbsp white wine vinegar
2 cloves garlic, pressed
½ tsp salt
1 tsp dry tarragon leaves
2 tbsp salad oil
1 (1½ to 1¾ pounds) salmon fillet

Although Marsha says friends know her for desserts, she enjoys cooking a variety of dishes. "I like it best in the summer when we can cook outside," she says.

1. In small saucepan, combine all ingredients, except salmon fillet. Bring to a simmer. Remove from heat, cover and let stand 1 hour.

2. Place salmon in shallow glass baking dish. Pour marinade over, cover and chill 30 minutes to 1 hour. Turn occasionally.

3. Prepare barbecue grill for medium-high heat; when coals are gray, remove salmon from marinade and place on grill, skin-side down. (If desired, use a fish grill basket.)

4. Grill 5 to 7 minutes, then turn. Grill 5 to 7 minutes more, depending on thickness, until fish flakes. Carefully remove from grill, and serve at once.

Makes 6 to 8 servings

Spicy Sesame Noodles
Patricia Johnson and Mark Wourms, Kansas City, Missouri

Mark, who is director of the Kansas City Zoo, goes with his instincts when he cooks, but his wife, Patricia, a dietitian, needs a recipe. They share a taste for spicy foods such as these sesame noodles.

1. In a small skillet or saucepan over medium heat, heat vegetable oil, and sauté green onions, garlic, ginger and chili peppers until garlic is soft but not brown, 3 to 4 minutes.

2. Turn off heat and add vinegar, soy sauce, sugar, peanut butter and ⅓ cup chicken stock. Turn on heat and simmer sauce, stirring 2 minutes. Add more chicken stock if necessary to achieve consistency of a cream sauce. Stir in the sesame oil.

3. Cook noodles according to package directions; drain. Add sauce. Toss to combine. Chill.

4. If desired, add cucumber and carrot strips and sprinkle sesame seeds over noodles for garnish.

Makes 4 to 5 servings

1½ tbsp vegetable oil
3 green onions, white parts only, minced
3 cloves garlic, minced
½-inch piece fresh ginger, minced (about 2 tsp)
2 small, dried Asian chili peppers, snipped with scissors
3½ tsp Chinese red vinegar, or 3 tsp rice vinegar
1 tbsp soy sauce
1 tbsp sugar
½ cup peanut butter
⅓ to ½ cup chicken stock, or chicken broth
1 tsp sesame oil
10 ounces fresh Chinese wheat or egg noodles, or ½ pound fettucine

Optional:
Cucumber, cut into matchsticks
Carrot, cut into matchsticks
1 tbsp sesame seeds

Penne Pasta con Broccoli

George Fry, Overland Park, Kansas

2 tbsp butter
2 tsp minced garlic
1½ cups fresh sliced mushrooms
1 bunch fresh broccoli, cut into
    flowerets
½ cup favorite tomato-based
    spaghetti sauce
2 cups heavy cream
1 pound penne pasta, cooked al
    dente and drained
1 cup grated Parmesan cheese

The Fry family schedule makes meals with the whole family a treat. This recipe is the kind George likes to fix on such occasions.

1. Melt butter in large (4- to 5-quart) heavy skillet over medium heat. When hot, add garlic, mushrooms and broccoli. Stir-fry 5 to 7 minutes, until mushrooms are slightly softened.

2. Add spaghetti sauce. Reduce heat to low and add cream, stirring constantly.

3. Add pasta and simmer 5 minutes, until heated through and cream is largely absorbed. Add Parmesan cheese and stir. Serve at once.

Makes about 8 servings

96

Pumpkin Kibbe

Mary Brown, Kansas City, Missouri

After a stint working as a cook in a Middle Eastern restaurant in Kansas, Mary now makes Middle Eastern food a standard in the Brown household. "I enjoy exploring ethnic foods," she says.

1. Preheat oven to 350 degrees. Combine pumpkin, bulgur, flour, green onions, orange peel, mint, marjoram, basil, thyme, salt, allspice, cayenne and black pepper. Set aside.

2. Make filling: Sauté onion in 2 tablespoons butter in pan over medium heat until softened, about 5 minutes. Add pine nuts, allspice, salt and black pepper, and sauté for another 1 to 2 minutes until slightly toasted.

3. Butter a 9- by 13-inch baking pan with 1 tablespoon butter. Using hands, pat down ½ of pumpkin mixture in bottom. Spread with onion filling. Pat down the rest of the pumpkin. Score top diagonally to form diamond shapes.

4. Melt remaining 2 tablespoons butter and drizzle over the top. Bake about 50 minutes, until golden brown and fairly firm. Serve with yogurt-garlic mixture.

Makes 12 servings

1 (29 oz) can pumpkin, or 3½ cups cooked pumpkin
2 cups fine grain bulgur wheat, soaked in cool water until soft (20 to 30 minutes), drained and squeezed of excess moisture
½ cup whole-wheat flour
4 green onions, including tender green tops, finely sliced
Grated peel of 1 orange
¼ cup finely chopped fresh mint
1 tbsp fresh marjoram
1 tbsp fresh minced basil
1 tbsp fresh minced thyme
1 tsp salt
1 tsp allspice
¼ tsp cayenne pepper
Freshly ground black pepper, to taste

For filling and topping:
1 large onion, chopped
5 tbsp butter, divided
½ cup pine nuts, plus more for optional garnish
1 tsp allspice
Salt and ground black pepper, to taste
2 cups plain yogurt blended with 1 minced or pressed clove garlic, ½ tsp ground black pepper and salt to taste

Spinach and Orzo

Diana Cozad, Leavenworth, Kansas

2 beaten eggs
3 cups cooked (1½ cups uncooked)
   orzo (rice-shaped pasta; other
   very small pasta may be
   substituted if orzo isn't available)
1 (15.5 oz) jar chunky spaghetti
   sauce, divided
½ cup grated Parmesan cheese
2 (10 oz) packages frozen chopped
   spinach
1 cup ricotta cheese
½ tsp ground nutmeg
½ tsp salt
1 cup shredded mozzarella cheese

1. Combine eggs, cooked orzo, ½ cup spaghetti sauce and Parmesan cheese.

2. Spread mixture over bottom and up sides of a greased 9- by 13-inch casserole dish to form a shell.

3. Cook spinach according to package directions; drain well. Stir together spinach, ricotta cheese, nutmeg and salt. Spread over pasta. Spread remaining spaghetti sauce over filling. Cover edge of pasta with foil.

4. Bake at 350 degrees 30 minutes, or until bubbly and edges are slightly brown. Remove from oven. Top with shredded mozzarella cheese.

5. Return to oven, and bake 3 to 5 minutes more, or until cheese has melted. Let stand on wire rack 5 minutes before serving.

Makes 10 servings

Eggplant Sandwich

Katie Hamilton, Overland Park, Kansas

Katie creates her own recipes, such as this one, based on the flavors of her father's Italian cooking.

1. Slice eggplant ¼-inch thick. Brush with olive oil on both sides. Grill over low to medium coals, turning once, until golden brown on both sides, 5 to 7 minutes total.

2. Cut bread in half lengthwise. Spread pesto on cut faces of bread. Place eggplant, cheese, mild peppers and optional tomato in layers on one half of loaf. Top with other half of loaf.

3. If desired, wrap loaf in foil and heat at 350 degrees 20 minutes. Cut crosswise into 4 sandwiches and serve.

Makes 4 servings

1 large eggplant
¼ cup olive oil
1 long loaf crusty French bread
¼ cup pesto (recipe follows)
¼ pound provolone cheese, thinly sliced
6 sliced mild peppers, such as banana peppers
1 fresh tomato, optional

Pesto

Katie Hamilton, Overland Park, Kansas

1. Place 4 cups basil in blender or food processor.

2. Add garlic, Romano cheese, pine nuts, oil and salt. Process until smooth, scraping down sides of container if necessary to puree all the basil.

3. Add remaining 2 cups basil leaves, and process until mixture is fairly smooth. Pesto should be thick, but it may be necessary to add more oil to achieve a spreadable consistency.

4. Taste and correct seasoning.

Makes about 2 cups

6 cups fresh basil leaves, divided
4 to 5 cloves garlic, according to taste
⅔ cup freshly grated Romano cheese
½ cup pine nuts
About 1 cup olive oil
Salt, to taste

Sun-Dried Tomato Pesto

Tom Klingner, Roeland Park, Kansas

1 cup reconstituted sun-dried
  tomatoes (reconstituted in water)
½ cup kalamata olives, pitted
1 large clove garlic, finely minced
1 very small white onion, finely
  chopped
½ tsp minced fresh thyme
¼ tsp red pepper flakes
½ cup plus 1 tbsp extra-virgin
  olive oil
12 ounces linguine
3 tbsp freshly grated Parmigiano
  Reggiano cheese, plus more for
  serving
1 tbsp unsalted butter
¼ cup fresh Italian parsley

Tom and his wife, Andrea, especially enjoy Italian food, and many Italian dishes, such as Sun-Dried Tomato Pesto, are quick and simple enough for week-night meals.

1. Coarsely chop the tomatoes. Finely chop the olives. In a bowl, combine the tomatoes, olives, garlic, onion, thyme and red pepper flakes. Add olive oil; mix thoroughly with a wooden spoon.

2. Cook pasta according to package directions; drain, reserving about ½ cup water. Transfer to warm bowl; toss with cheese, butter and parsley.

3. Add 2 tablespoons hot pasta water to the pesto. Toss the pesto with the pasta and serve. Pass additional Parmigiano Reggiano.

Note: This robust sauce makes an interesting accompaniment to grilled tuna.

Makes 3 to 4 servings

Tofu Vegetarian

Kathy Kuhlmann, Lake Waukomis, Missouri

Korean food typically is spicy. You can tone down the spice in Tofu Vegetarian by reducing the amount of red pepper. (This pepper isn't as hot as cayenne. If substituting cayenne for the Oriental pepper, start with a small amount of cayenne and add a little at a time until the dish is quite hot or to your taste.)

1. Arrange tofu, mushrooms, onions, potatoes and carrots in strips in large, cold frying pan.

2. In bowl, mix soy sauce, garlic, sesame oil, water, black pepper and red pepper. Pour over vegetables.

3. Turn heat under pan to high. Bring to a boil, reduce heat to medium, cover and cook 10 minutes or until vegetables are tender. Transfer to serving plate, maintaining the separate lines of tofu, mushrooms, etc. Serve with steamed rice.

Note: Shredded dried mushrooms are sold in Oriental groceries. If shredded variety isn't available, buy dried sliced Oriental mushrooms and soak them 20 minutes in water. Squeeze excess moisture from mushrooms and chop.

Makes 4 to 6 servings

1 (10½ oz) package tofu, cut in ½-inch cubes
½ ounce shredded dried mushrooms (see note)
1 medium onion, cut in half lengthwise and sliced crosswise to make semi-circular slices.
1 large potato, cut in half lengthwise and sliced crosswise
½ carrot, shredded
¼ cup soy sauce
3 cloves garlic, minced
2 tbsp sesame oil
¼ cup water
¼ tsp freshly ground black pepper
2 tbsp Oriental ground red pepper, or to taste

Pasta with Herbed Tomatoes and Cheese

Merrill Myers, Mission Woods, Kansas

8 medium tomatoes, peeled, seeded and coarsely chopped
4 cloves garlic, minced
1 cup fresh basil, chopped
2 tbsp chopped fresh mint
2 tsp salt
1 tsp freshly ground black pepper, plus more for garnish
¾ tsp red pepper flakes

½ cup olive oil
1 pound small pasta shells, or rotini
½ cup freshly grated Parmesan cheese
½ pound Fontina cheese, finely diced (about 2 cups)

"Probably we eat more Italian food than anything else, plus it's something the kids will eat," Merrill says.

1. In a large serving bowl, toss together tomatoes, garlic, basil, mint, salt, 1 teaspoon black pepper, red pepper and olive oil. Let stand at room temperature at least 2 to 3 hours, tossing occasionally.

2. Cook pasta according to package directions until al dente. While pasta is cooking, add Parmesan cheese and Fontina to tomato mixture. Drain and transfer pasta to the tomato-cheese mixture in serving bowl. Toss until combined.

3. Garnish as desired with additional black pepper. Serve warm or at room temperature.

Note: Best served fresh. Doesn't store well.

Makes 6 to 8 servings

Black Bean Burritos

Nancy O'Connor, Lawrence, Kansas

"A lot of people want to move away from eating red meat every day, but it can be a big leap from a steak to a plate of beans," says Nancy. Her goal as a nutrition educator is to provide ideas on how to fill the breach.

1. Heat the black beans, then spread ⅓ to ½ cup beans down the center of each tortilla. Top with 2 to 3 tablespoons grated cheese. Roll up tortilla, and place in 9- by 13-inch baking dish.

2. When all burritos are in dish, spread remaining cheese on top, and bake at 350 degrees 15 to 20 minutes, or until cheese is bubbly and tortillas are lightly browned.

3. Garnish with cucumber, tomatoes, onion, lettuce, yogurt and salsa. If you have guacamole, use it, too. This is a quick, colorful and tasty dish.

Makes 8 servings

3 cups cooked, seasoned black beans
8 large flour tortillas
2 cups grated cheese, such as low-fat Jack, Colby or cheddar
1 cucumber, chopped
2 medium tomatoes, chopped
½ onion, chopped
2 cups shredded lettuce
8 ounces plain yogurt
Salsa, to taste
Guacamole (optional)

Southwest Casserole

Doug Worgul, Lenexa, Kansas

2 cups dry black or red beans, soaked
  overnight in water
4 to 5 (14.5 oz) cans low-sodium
  chicken broth, divided
1 cup uncooked brown rice
⅓ cup uncooked wild rice
4 (16 oz) cans diced tomatoes,
  drained
Jalapeno peppers, to taste
1 red bell pepper, diced
1 yellow onion, chopped very fine
Green tops from 1 bunch green
  onions, chopped fine
2 cloves garlic, chopped fine
1 (16 oz) can corn
2½ tsp ground cayenne pepper
2 tsp ground cumin
Freshly ground black pepper to taste
Salt to taste
Grated Monterey Jack and sharp
  cheddar cheese

Doug's family has a history of heart disease and high-fat eating. It is a history Doug is determined not to repeat. "For me, that means meals that concentrate more on fruits and vegetables and carbohydrates than on meat," he says.

1. Drain beans. Place them in pot with 2 to 3 cans of chicken broth (enough for the beans to move freely). Bring to a boil; cover and simmer about 1 hour, or until firm (neither hard nor mushy).

2. In a separate pan, bring 2⅔ cups chicken broth to boil, stir in the brown rice and wild rice; reduce heat to low, cover and cook to desired tenderness, about 1 hour.

3. When rice and beans are done, combine them thoroughly. Add remaining ingredients, except cheese, mixing well.

4. Transfer to 2-quart baking dish, and bake at 325 degrees 1 hour, or until heated through. Serve, topped with grated cheese.

Makes 6 servings

Side Dishes
Vegetables, Potatoes & Rice

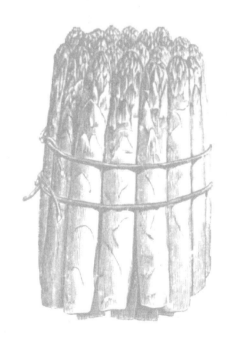

Vegetables

Green Beans with Balsamic-Glazed Onions

Laura Gault Welch, Weatherby Lake, Missouri

Laura's flavorful green bean dish is from a menu she developed for a Christmas dinner.

2 pounds fresh pearl onions, or
    2 (1-pound) bags frozen pearl
    onions, thawed
½ cup balsamic vinegar, divided
2 tbsp unsalted butter
2 tbsp vegetable oil
2 tsp finely chopped fresh thyme, or
    1 tsp dried thyme
1½ tsp freshly ground black pepper,
    divided
1 tsp salt, divided
3 pounds fresh green beans, trimmed
¼ cup mild olive oil
1 tbsp Dijon mustard

1. In a large saucepan of boiling water, blanch the fresh onions 1 minute. Drain and refresh under cold running water; drain. Using a small, sharp knife, trim the root ends and slip off the skins. (If using thawed onions, no further preparation is required.)

2. Preheat oven to 400 degrees. In a small nonreactive saucepan, combine ¼ cup of balsamic vinegar, butter, vegetable oil, thyme, 1 teaspoon black pepper and ½ teaspoon salt; stir over moderately low heat until butter is melted.

3. In a medium bowl, toss the onions with vinegar mixture to coat. Spread the onions in a single layer on a baking sheet, and bake at 400 degrees 35 to 40 minutes, stirring often, until evenly browned.

4. Meanwhile, in a large pot of boiling, salted water, blanch the green beans until just tender, about 4 minutes. Drain and refresh under cold running water; drain and set aside.

5. In a large bowl, combine olive oil, mustard and remaining ¼ cup balsamic vinegar and remaining ½ teaspoon each of salt and black pepper. Add the green beans and the onions to the dressing in the bowl, and toss well.

6. Transfer the vegetables to a large (3- to 4-quart) casserole, and cover.

7. Reduce oven heat to 350 degrees, and bake vegetables about 20 minutes, or until heated through.

Adapted from *Food & Wine* magazine.

Note: To prepare up to a day ahead, prepare through Step 6, and refrigerate covered casserole. When ready to use, bring casserole to room temperature and bake as directed in Step 7.

Makes 8 to 10 servings

Mamie's Italian Green Beans

Robert and Sara Jenkins, Kansas City, Missouri

1. In small skillet over medium-low heat, cook onion and garlic in olive oil until lightly browned.

2. Add green beans and artichoke hearts. Stir and heat thoroughly. Reduce to simmer. Add bread crumbs, Parmesan cheese and red pepper flakes. Stir until beans are well coated. Remove from heat.

3. Cover; set aside a few minutes before serving.

Variation: Substitute 3 cups fresh, peeled, chopped zucchini for beans and artichoke hearts.

Makes 4 to 6 servings

½ cup finely chopped onion
1 tsp minced garlic
2 tbsp olive oil
1 (16 oz) can French-style green beans, drained
½ cup coarsely chopped marinated artichoke hearts
½ cup seasoned bread crumbs
¼ cup grated Parmesan cheese
Red pepper flakes or Tabasco sauce, to taste

Cashew Green Beans

Candy Linn, Prairie Village, Kansas

½ cup coarsely chopped salted
  cashews
3 tbsp unsalted butter
2 tbsp honey
1 pound fresh green beans, blanched
  and drained

1. Cook cashews in butter over low heat about 5 minutes.

2. Add honey and cook 1 minute longer, stirring constantly.

3. Pour sauce over beans and toss until coated.

This recipe doubles easily.

Makes 4 servings

Raspberry Marinated Carrots

Patricia Speier and Andrew Green, Overland Park, Kansas

1½ pounds carrots
⅓ cup raspberry vinegar
About ½ cup extra-virgin olive oil
Freshly ground black pepper, to taste

1. Peel and cut carrots into ⅛-inch-thick coins. Bring a pot of salted water to a boil, and drop in carrots. Cook about 6 minutes, or until al dente.

2. Drain carrots and place in a bowl. While carrots are still hot, sprinkle with raspberry vinegar. Add enough olive oil to coat; toss well. Refrigerate at least overnight.

3. Bring carrots to room temperature and lift them from marinade with a slotted spoon before serving. Season generously with black pepper.

Makes 6 servings

Vegetable Grill

Donna and Dennis Poppe, Olathe, Kansas

This recipe takes advantage of Dennis's bountiful garden produce. "You get real creative when you have two garbage bags full of broccoli," Donna says.

1. Cut zucchini lengthwise into quarters. Cut onion into ½-inch-thick slices. Cut mushrooms and tomatoes in half. Cut green pepper into slices or chunks.

2. Place all the vegetables, including broccoli, on jelly roll pan small enough to fit on grill. Brush vegetables with olive oil and sprinkle with fajita seasoning or other seasonings of your choice. Cover pan with foil and place about 3 inches from medium coals.

3. Cook, stirring occasionally to ensure even cooking and to avoid sticking, about 10 minutes, or until crisp-tender. (If desired, cook alongside meat, starting with hot coals to sear meat, then regulating to medium temperature for rest of cooking time.)

Note: You can vary vegetables according to availability.

Makes 4 servings

2 zucchini squash, 8 to 10 inches long
1 large onion
10 to 15 whole mushrooms
4 Roma tomatoes
1 green pepper
1 large stalk broccoli, cut into flowerets
Olive oil
Dry fajita seasoning, or salt, ground black pepper, garlic salt, spices and other seasonings, to taste

Roasted Asparagus with Brown Butter

Diana Phillips, Kansas City, Missouri

3 tbsp butter
3 pounds asparagus
1 tbsp olive oil
¾ tsp salt
½ tsp freshly ground black pepper

Diana and her friend, Cori Osborn, led the effort to create a cookbook to help raise funds for the Kansas City Community Kitchen, a nonprofit group that serves free meals to the needy. This recipe was one of Diana's contributions.

1. Preheat oven to 450 degrees. Meanwhile, in a small saucepan, melt butter over moderate heat, and cook until golden brown, about 2 minutes. Immediately remove pan from heat but keep warm. When cooking butter, watch closely to avoid burning. If butter starts to smoke, throw it out, wash pan and start again.

2. Snap off tough ends of asparagus and discard. On a large baking sheet, toss asparagus with olive oil, salt and black pepper. Spread asparagus on the baking sheet and roast in just until tender, 5 to 12 minutes, depending on thickness of the spears. Asparagus can be cooked on hot grill until marked but still firm.

3. Transfer asparagus to platter or individual serving plates, and pour brown butter over. Serve immediately.

Makes 6 to 8 servings

Carrots Glazed with Honey and Brandy

Ed Dobbins, Fairway, Kansas

1. Combine carrots, water, sugar, salt and 3 tablespoons butter in large heavy saucepan.

2. Bring to a boil. Reduce heat, cover and simmer until carrots are crisp-tender, about 10 minutes. Drain well.

3. Place remaining 3 tablespoons butter, honey and brown sugar in large, heavy skillet over medium-high heat; cook, stirring, until butter melts and sugar dissolves. Reduce heat to low.

4. Add carrots and brandy; cook and toss until carrots are coated with glaze, about 3 minutes. Sprinkle with parsley and serve.

Makes 10 servings

3 pounds carrots, peeled and cut diagonally into 1/4-inch-thick slices
2 cups water
2 tbsp sugar
1 tsp salt
6 tbsp unsalted butter, divided
3 tbsp honey
1 1/2 tbsp brown sugar, or to taste
3 tbsp brandy
3 tbsp chopped fresh parsley

Okra and Tomato Gumbo

Jessie Cooperwood, Grandview, Missouri

1. Bring water to a boil.

2. Add onions; cook 5 minutes.

3. Add remaining ingredients, and simmer about 45 minutes, or until okra is very tender. Serve over rice.

Makes 8 to 10 servings

3/4 cup water
1 medium onion, chopped
1 (12 oz) package frozen okra, cut or whole
1 (16 oz) can crushed tomatoes
1 tbsp butter
Salt substitute or other seasoning, to taste

"Fresh" Creamed Corn

Beth Legler, Blue Springs, Missouri

1 (20 oz) package frozen whole
    kernel corn, partially thawed
3 tbsp butter
3 tbsp sugar
1/4 tsp salt
1/8 tsp ground black pepper
2/3 cup milk

1. Place corn in food processor with metal blade. Process 30 seconds to 1 minute, or until half the corn kernels are pureed. (You should have some whole corn kernels remaining.)

2. Melt butter in large, heavy skillet. Add corn and remaining ingredients. Stir. Cover and cook over low heat 15 to 20 minutes, until liquid is reduced to creamed corn consistency. Stir occasionally. More milk may be added if mixture becomes too dry. Serve hot.

Variation: To prepare dish in advance, transfer the combined ingredients to a 1 1/2-quart casserole dish. Cover and refrigerate until 45 minutes before ready to serve. Then bake, covered, at 300 degrees 30 to 45 minutes until heated through.

Adapted from *Sassafras.*

Makes 6 servings

Sugar Snap Peas with Sesame Seeds

Russ and Donamae Rebman, Leawood, Kansas

2 tbsp sesame seeds
2 tbsp butter
4 cups fresh sugar snap peas, cleaned
Freshly ground black pepper, to taste

1. Toast sesame seeds in dry skillet. Set aside.

2. Melt butter; add peas, and sauté over medium heat under tender, about 3 minutes.

3. Stir in sesame seeds, and season with black pepper. Serve at once.

Makes 8 servings

Veggie Tortilla

Pamela and Buddy Kruger, Lake Winnebago, Missouri

Eating isn't what it used to be at the Kruger household. It's lighter, healthier and much longer on vegetables.

1. Heat water about ½-inch deep in nonstick skillet over medium-high heat. Add carrots, green onions, zucchini, squash, garlic, red pepper, salt, black pepper, cilantro and celery salt. Cook and stir 5 to 7 minutes, or until just tender.

2. Place ⅙ of cheese on each tortilla; place tortilla on baking sheet. Heat in toaster oven or under broiler until cheese is just melted.

3. Spread vegetables on top of cheese. Sprinkle with Spike seasoning.

Variation: To make without cheese, warm tortillas in hot, dry skillet before spreading with vegetables.

Makes 6 servings

¼ to ½ cup water
2 carrots, chopped
4 green onions, chopped
½ zucchini, chopped
½ yellow squash, sliced
3 cloves garlic, minced
¼ red bell pepper, sliced
⅛ tsp salt
⅛ tsp ground black pepper
⅛ tsp dried cilantro
⅛ tsp celery salt
1 cup shredded Monterey Jack cheese
6 soft corn tortillas
Spike, or similar herb-seasoned salt,
    to taste

Niangua River Potatoes

Debbie Geraghty and Susie Miller, Lenexa, Kansas

6 refrigerated baked potatoes, skin on
¼ cup margarine
Salt and ground black pepper, to taste

Sisters Debbie and Susie made these potatoes as a variation of their grandfather's deep-fried version.

1. Cut potatoes in ¼-inch slices.

2. Heat margarine in large skillet over medium heat. Brown potatoes in hot margarine till crispy, stirring occasionally.

3. Add salt and black pepper to taste, and serve.

Makes 6 servings

Patate Abruzzesi (Abruzzi-Style Potatoes)

Mary Beth Ricci, Olathe, Kansas

3 pounds new potatoes, unpeeled
   and scrubbed
½ tsp hot red pepper flakes
2 tbsp fresh rosemary leaves
3 cloves garlic, minced
¼ cup olive oil

1. Preheat oven to 400 degrees. Cut potatoes into thick pieces.

2. Sprinkle red pepper flakes, rosemary, garlic and olive oil over potatoes, and toss to mix well.

3. Put into a roasting pan and roast about 1 hour, or until browned, turning occasionally. Serve hot.

Makes 6 servings

Lemon Potatoes

Arlene Horning, Shawnee, Kansas

1. Peel potatoes, and slice about ¼-inch thick. Parboil in lightly salted water 5 to 10 minutes, or until barely tender. (Potatoes should still be slightly crisp.) Drain.

2. While potatoes are cooking, combine butter, sugar, lemon juice and basil in a large, heavy skillet. Heat slowly, about 5 minutes, stirring constantly, until butter is melted and resulting syrup is bubbly.

3. Add drained potatoes to syrup, and cook over low heat 10 to 15 minutes, until potatoes are nicely glazed. Spoon syrup over potatoes often while cooking.

4. To serve, sprinkle with grated lemon rind.

Makes about 6 servings

2 pounds red potatoes (6 to 8 medium potatoes)
½ cup (1 stick) butter
½ cup sugar
1 tbsp lemon juice
1 tsp dried basil
Grated lemon peel

Stovies (Scottish Skillet Potatoes)

Scott Murray, Kansas City, Missouri

2 tbsp bacon fat, butter or margarine
6 medium potatoes, sliced ¼-inch
    thick with skins on, divided
2 medium onions, sliced ¼- to ½-
    inch thick, divided
½ tsp ground black pepper, divided
¼ cup snipped parsley, or 2 to 3 tbsp
    dried parsley, divided
¼ tsp salt, or to taste, divided
¾ cup water

Scott recommends Stovies as a dish you can get on the stove in 15 minutes and forget for the 30 minutes it takes to cook. The recipe is based on one in *Betty Crocker's International Cookbook* (1980).

1. In large skillet, melt fat, and coat bottom and sides of skillet. Layer half of potatoes and onions in pan, then sprinkle with half the black pepper, parsley and salt.

2. Repeat with remaining potatoes, onions, black pepper, parsley and salt.

3. Add water. Bring almost to a boil, cover, reduce heat to low, and simmer about 30 minutes until potatoes are tender, and water is absorbed. If water is absorbed before potatoes are done, add a bit more water.

Makes 6 servings

Sweet Potatoes

Eula Brooks, Kansas City, Missouri

Eula loves to cook traditional foods, and she likes to add her own touches, as she did with these sweet potatoes.

1. In bowl, combine hot mashed sweet potatoes, milk, butter, sugar, vanilla, beaten eggs and nutmeg.

2. Mix well and spread in 11¾- by 7½-inch baking dish.

3. For topping: Mix together melted butter, brown sugar and flour. Add pecans, and sprinkle over potatoes.

4. Bake at 350 degrees 25 minutes, or until firm or knife inserted in center comes out clean.

Makes 6 servings

3 cups pared, cooked and mashed
  sweet potatoes
½ cup milk
½ cup (1 stick) butter
1½ cups sugar
1 tsp vanilla
2 eggs, beaten
½ tsp nutmeg

For topping:
⅓ cup melted butter
1 cup brown sugar
½ cup all-purpose flour
1 cup pecans, chopped

Easy Microwave Potatoes

Doris Wilson, Kansas City, Missouri

Doris cooked up this recipe one evening when she didn't want plain baked potatoes.

1. Place potatoes in microwave dish. Sprinkle with salt, black pepper and parsley. Add water and margarine.

2. Place plastic wrap over dish and cook on high 10 minutes. Stir, reseal and cook on high 5 more minutes, or until tender.

Variation: Top with cheese slices before final 5 minutes of cooking.

Makes 4 servings

4 medium red potatoes, peeled and
  sliced ¼-inch thick
Salt and black pepper, to taste
Parsley flakes, to taste
¼ cup water
½ stick margarine, sliced

Risotto alla Milanese

Gina Valente, Mission, Kansas

7 cups chicken stock
4 tbsp butter
½ cup finely chopped onion
⅓ to ½ cup chopped uncooked beef
    marrow, optional
2 cups Arborio rice (plain imported
    short-grain Italian rice)
⅛ tsp powdered saffron, optional
4 tbsp soft butter
½ cup freshly grated imported
    Parmesan cheese

Risotto, a creamy-textured dish made from short-grained Arborio rice, results from slow cooking and stirring the rice to help it absorb more than the usual amount of liquid. Gina says, "What is good about risotto is that you can add mushrooms or shrimp to it, or serve it this way as a meal or a side dish."

1. Bring chicken stock to a simmer in a 2- to 3-quart saucepan, and keep it barely simmering over low heat.

2. In a heavy 3-quart flameproof casserole, melt 4 tablespoons of butter over moderate heat. Cook onions in butter, stirring frequently, 7 to 8 minutes. Do not let onions brown.

3. Stir in the optional marrow, then add rice and cook, stirring, 1 to 2 minutes, or until rice glistens and is somewhat opaque.

4. Add stock to cover and cook, stirring continuously, until stock is almost completely absorbed. Add more stock to cover and continue cooking as before.

5. Repeat until you have used all but about 2 cups of stock. Add optional saffron to the 2 cups of stock and let it steep a few minutes, then add stock to cooking rice as before. When all stock is completely absorbed, rice should be tender. If it is still firm, add more stock, ½ cup at a time, and continue cooking and stirring until the rice is soft.

6. Stir in 4 tablespoons soft butter and grated cheese with a fork, taking care not to mash the rice. Garnish with a sprig of fresh parsley and serve while rice is creamy and piping hot.

Makes 6 to 8 servings

Tortilla Espanola

Jeff Seybert, Shawnee, Kansas

Like many of Jeff's favorite dishes, this one has a healthy dose of garlic.

1. Sauté onion in 1 tablespoon olive oil over medium heat until nearly soft, about 3 minutes; add garlic and continue cooking 1 to 2 minutes to soften garlic. Set aside to cool.

2. Beat eggs in large bowl; add salt and black pepper to taste, and stir in onion mixture.

3. Heat remaining 3 tablespoons olive oil in nonstick skillet over medium heat. Add potatoes and sauté, stirring frequently, until cooked through but not browned (some slight browning may occur). Set aside to cool.

4. Add cooled potatoes to egg mixture, and gently stir until ingredients are well mixed. Let mixture sit 15 minutes.

5. Lightly coat a deep-dish (9-inch) glass pie pan with olive oil or nonstick cooking spray. Pour mixture into pan, and bake at 375 degrees 30 to 40 minutes, until golden brown and tester inserted in center comes out clean.

6. Gently loosen edges of tortilla with a spatula and let cool. Invert a serving plate on top of pie plate, and turn the tortilla out upside down onto the serving plate.

Makes 4 to 6 side-dish servings, 8 to 12 appetizer servings

4 tbsp good quality olive oil, divided
1 large onion, coarsely chopped
4 to 6 cloves garlic, according to taste, minced
6 large eggs
Salt and black pepper, to taste
6 large potatoes, sliced thin (about ⅛ inch) with skin on or off as preferred

Creole Rice Pilaf

Dot Wade, Kansas City, Missouri

2¼ cups chicken broth
¼ cup white wine
½ cup (1 stick) butter, divided
1 cup uncooked brown rice
¼ cup chopped onion
Salt to taste
1¼ cups fresh mushrooms sliced or
    cut into chunks
½ tsp chopped garlic
2 tomatoes, peeled and chopped
½ tsp oregano
Black pepper to taste
1 tsp lemon juice
½ tsp dried parsley
1 ripe avocado, sliced

1. In saucepan, combine chicken broth, wine and 6 tablespoons butter. Bring to a boil. Add rice and onion, and season with salt to taste. Cover tightly and cook over low heat about 50 minutes, or until water is absorbed.

2. In another pan, melt remaining 2 tablespoons butter and sauté mushrooms just to heat through. Stir in garlic, tomatoes and oregano. Season to taste with salt and black pepper and lemon juice.

3. Add mushroom mixture, parsley and sliced avocado to rice, and toss gently.

Makes 6 servings

Sweet Finishes
Cookies, Cakes, Pies, Pastries & Desserts

Cookies

Ranger Cookies

Nancy Long, Overland Park, Kansas

½ cup shortening
½ cup sugar
½ cup packed brown sugar
1 egg
½ tsp vanilla
1 cup all-purpose flour
½ tsp baking soda
¼ tsp baking powder
¼ tsp salt
1 cup quick-cooking oats
1 cup Wheaties or Total cereal
½ cup shredded coconut

Nancy grew up with Ranger Cookies and has made the recipe for years.

1. Heat oven to 375 degrees.

2. In mixing bowl, thoroughly mix shortening, sugar, brown sugar, egg and vanilla.

3. Stir in flour, baking soda, baking powder, salt, oats, cereal and coconut.

4. Drop by rounded teaspoonfuls 2 inches apart on ungreased baking sheet. Bake 10 minutes, or until set. Immediately remove to wire rack. Take care not to overcook, or cookies will be hard.

Makes 3 dozen

Oatmeal–Rice Krispie Cookies

Jane Shearer, Kansas City, Kansas

Jane enjoys all kinds of cooking, but when she picks out her favorite recipes, baked goods show up in disproportionate numbers.

1. Blend margarine and sugar; add egg and vanilla. Stir in dry ingredients.

2. Roll mixture into walnut-size balls. Place about 2 inches apart on ungreased baking sheet. Press down with bottom of glass dipped in sugar, forming circles 1/4- to 1/2-inch thick.

3. Bake at 350 degrees 10 to 12 minutes, until lightly browned.

Makes 4 to 5 dozen

1 cup margarine
1 cup sugar
1 egg
1 tsp vanilla
1 1/2 cups all-purpose flour
1/4 tsp baking soda
1/4 tsp cream of tartar
1/2 tsp salt, optional
1 cup crisp rice cereal, such as Rice Krispies
1 cup quick-cooking oatmeal

Gordon's Favorite Hazelnut and Chocolate Chip Biscotti

Sally Slabotsky, Shawnee Mission, Kansas

4 cups all-purpose flour
2 cups sugar
2 tsp baking powder
1 tsp baking soda
4 eggs
4 tbsp Frangelico (hazelnut liqueur)
2 tsp almond extract
2 tsp vanilla
1½ cups hazelnuts, coarsely chopped
½ cup chocolate chips

Sally says pleasing her family is her primary concern: "Cooking is something we all share. We love to exchange recipes."

1. Using electric mixer with paddle attachment, mix flour, sugar, baking powder and baking soda until well combined.

2. In separate bowl, combine eggs, Frangelico, almond extract and vanilla. With mixer at low speed, pour liquid mixture into dry mixture; mix until dough is well-combined. Stir in hazelnuts and chocolate chips.

3. Shape dough into logs about 3 inches wide and a length that fits your baking sheet. Place on greased baking sheet.

4. Bake in preheated oven at 350 degrees 25 minutes, or until lightly browned.

5. Remove from oven and cool on pans. Slice, diagonally, about ½-inch wide with serrated knife or electric knife.

6. Lay slices on ungreased baking sheet; bake again at 300 degrees about 15 minutes, turning once, until golden brown on both sides.

Makes about 40 pieces

Double Peanut Butter Cookies

Teresa Watson, Overland Park, Kansas

This recipe works well when doubled (as it usually is at the Watson household).

1. Sift together flour, sugar, baking soda and salt. Cut in shortening and peanut butter until mixture resembles a coarse meal. Blend in corn syrup and milk.

2. Shape into 2-inch log roll; cover with plastic wrap and chill about 1 hour.

3. Cut into slices ⅛- to ¼-inch thick.

4. Place half the slices at least 2 inches apart on ungreased baking sheet. Spread each with ½ teaspoon peanut butter. Cover with remaining slices; seal edges with fork.

5. Bake at 350 degrees 12 minutes, or until light golden. Cool on pan for 1 minute, then remove to racks to cool.

Makes 2½ dozen

1½ cups all-purpose flour
½ cup sugar
½ tsp baking soda
¼ tsp salt
½ cup shortening
½ cup creamy peanut butter, plus more for filling
¼ cup light corn syrup
1 tbsp milk

Almond Brittle Cookies

Laurie Bedlington, Kansas City, Missouri

For pastry:
½ cup (1 stick) butter
1 cup sugar
½ tsp salt
½ tsp vanilla
Grated rind of two oranges
1 egg
2 tbsp milk
1½ cups cake flour
1½ cups whole-wheat flour
½ cup raspberry jam (not dietetic)
1½ tbsp Cognac

For glazed-almond topping:
4 tbsp (½ stick) butter
½ cup sugar
½ tsp salt
2 tbsp honey
¼ cup cream, or milk
½ tsp vanilla
Juice of 1 lemon, strained
8 to 10 ounces sliced, blanched
   almonds

"I'm a purist," says Laurie. **"I'm not interested in cooking just for my health. Things taste good with butter and with olive oil."**

1. For pastry: Cream butter with an electric mixer. Gradually add sugar, beating constantly until mixture is thick and creamy.

2. Beat in salt, vanilla, orange rind, egg and milk. Add cake flour and whole-wheat flour, and beat at medium speed. Turn onto work surface. Shape into a ball, wrap and chill 1 to 2 hours.

3. Butter a 15- by 10- by 1-inch baking sheet, preferably a nonstick baking sheet.

4. Roll out pastry on a lightly floured board about 1 inch larger than baking sheet. Roll up pastry onto rolling pin. Center over baking sheet and unroll pastry. If pastry breaks, patch holes by pressing together with fingers. Prick pastry all over with a fork.

5. Bake at 350 degrees 12 to 15 minutes, checking after 5 minutes. If pastry is bubbling, prick again with a fork. When pastry is golden, remove from the oven and cool slightly. Increase oven temperature to 400 degrees.

6. Heat the jam to make it more spreadable. Stir in the Cognac. Brush or spoon a thin layer of jam over the pastry.

7. For topping: Melt butter over low heat. Stir in sugar, salt and honey. Continue stirring until sugar has melted. With heat still at low, add the cream and bring to a boil. Boil, stirring, until smooth and thickened, 2 to 3 minutes.

8. Remove from heat and stir in vanilla, lemon juice and almonds. Spread the mixture over the pastry.

9. Bake in a preheated oven at 400 degrees 12 to 15 minutes, or until golden.

10. Cool in pan. Cut into 1-inch squares.

Makes 40 to 50 cookies

Lemon Squares

Nancy Wagner, Kansas City, Missouri

1. Sift ½ cup confectioners' sugar with 2 cups flour. Cut in butter. Press mixture into lightly greased 10- by 14-inch jelly roll pan.

2. Bake at 350 degrees 20 minutes, or until lightly browned.

3. Beat together eggs and sugar. Add lemon juice and lemon rind; beat well. Stir in remaining ¼ cup flour and baking powder. Pour over baked crust.

4. Return to oven; bake at 350 degrees 25 minutes, or until set. Cool in pan. Sift confectioners' sugar over top. Cut into squares or bars, and serve.

Makes 3 dozen

½ cup confectioners' sugar, plus more for garnish
2¼ cups all-purpose flour, divided
1 cup (2 sticks) butter
4 eggs
2 cups sugar
⅓ cup lemon juice
1 tsp grated lemon rind, or to taste
½ tsp baking powder

Powdered Sugar Cookies

Mary Lickteig, Overland Park, Kansas

1 cup confectioners' sugar
2 cups all-purpose flour
1 tsp baking soda
1 tsp cream of tartar
½ cup vegetable shortening
½ cup butter, at room temperature
1 egg
2 tsp vanilla
Confectioners' Icing
Colored sugar, optional

This recipe is from Mary's Aunt Clara. The recipe is a favorite, not just for taste, but for the memories. "We used to get together with my aunt to make cookies, to make plates of cookies and take them to neighbors and friends," Mary recalls. "I have had other sugar cookies, but these taste so good."

1. Sift together in mixing bowl sugar, flour, baking soda and cream of tartar. Cut in shortening and butter with a pastry blender or fork until pieces are the size of peas.

2. In small bowl, combine egg and vanilla; add to flour mixture. Blend ingredients until a soft ball is formed.

3. Refrigerate at least 2 hours. Divide dough into 3 parts. Take 1 part at a time and flatten on lightly floured surface. Roll out with floured rolling pin from the center to the edge to a uniform ⅛-inch thickness.

4. Cut with cookie cutters and gently transfer to an ungreased baking sheet with a floured spatula.

5. Bake in 375-degree oven till lightly browned, 8 to 10 minutes. Frost with Confectioners' Icing (see recipe on page 155) when cool, and sprinkle with sugar.

Makes 3 to 4 dozen

Grandma Rydh's Wish Cookies

Barbara Bernardy, Blue Springs, Missouri

Place a cookie in the palm of your hand, face up, and make a wish. Break the cookie by tapping the center with the knuckle of the index finger of your other hand. If the cookie breaks into three pieces, you will get your wish. If it breaks into two pieces, you will have to wait a while for this wish. If it breaks into more than three pieces, you will need to be patient or change the wish before you can get it.

1. Cream together butter, 1 cup sugar and brown sugar. Add eggs, molasses and corn syrup; mix well.

2. Add flour, cloves, baking soda, baking powder, cinnamon and salt; mix well.

3. Chill dough 2 hours or overnight in refrigerator.

4. Roll dough into 1-inch balls; roll in sugar and place 2 inches apart on greased cookie sheets. Flatten to about ⅛ inch with the bottom of a glass dipped in sugar.

5. Bake at 350 degrees 8 to 10 minutes, or until slightly brown around edges. Remove immediately to waxed paper or cooling racks.

Makes 4 dozen

¾ cup (1½ sticks) butter
1 cup sugar, plus more to roll dough
1 cup brown sugar
3 eggs
¼ cup light molasses
¼ cup white corn syrup
4 cups all-purpose flour
2 tsp ground cloves
1 tsp baking soda
1 tsp baking powder
2 tsp cinnamon
1 tsp salt

Fudgy Saucepan Brownies

Abby Raynolds, Prairie Village, Kansas

¼ cup (½ stick) butter or margarine
¾ cup Prune Paste (recipe follows)
¾ cup cocoa
2¼ cups sugar
1 tsp vanilla
½ tsp salt
3 eggs
1¼ cups all-purpose flour
½ tsp baking powder
1 cup chopped nuts, optional

Abby savors her sweets, especially the chocolate ones. But Abby, a registered nurse, wants to cut fat where she can. She was delighted, then, when she found a "secret ingredient" to make many of her favorite desserts with a little less fat. The secret is Prune Paste. The surface of these prune-paste brownies often is sticky when removed from the oven, but the stickiness goes away when the brownies cool.

1. Melt butter over low heat, stir in Prune Paste and cocoa. Cool slightly.

2. Add sugar, vanilla, salt and eggs. Beat until combined, then add flour and baking powder; mix well. Stir in nuts, if desired.

3. Spread in greased 9- by 13-inch pan. Bake at 350 degrees about 30 minutes, or until toothpick inserted in center comes out clean.

Makes 12 to 16 large brownies

Prune Paste

1 cup pitted prunes
6 tbsp water
2 tsp vanilla

1. Combine all ingredients in food processor or blender. Blend until smooth.

2. Substitute for as much as 75 percent of the shortening in recipes for brownies, muffins and other baked goods. It is best used fresh, but can be kept in refrigerator several days.

Makes about 1 cup

Sour Cream Chocolate Cake

Wan Jean Bell, Kansas City, Missouri

This cake is one Wan Jean's mother used to make.

1. Grease and flour a 9- by 13-inch baking pan, 2 (9-inch) layer cake pans, 3 (8-inch) layer pans or 3 dozen cupcake tins (or line with paper).

2. Place all cake ingredients in large mixing bowl. Using an electric mixer, mix 30 seconds on low speed, then beat 3 minutes on high speed, scraping bowl constantly.

3. Pour batter into prepared pan or pans. Bake at 350 degrees 40 to 45 minutes in oblong pan, or 30 to 35 minutes in layer pans, or until toothpick inserted in center comes out clean. Bake cupcakes 20 to 25 minutes. Cool 5 minutes in pan, then remove to racks to cool completely.

4. To make frosting: Mix butter and chocolate until well-blended. Blend in sugar. Add sour cream and vanilla; beat until smooth. Frost cake.

Makes at least 20 servings

For cake:
2 cups all-purpose flour
2 cups sugar
1 cup water
¾ cup dairy sour cream
⅓ cup shortening
1¼ tsp baking soda
1 tsp salt
1 tsp vanilla
½ tsp baking powder
2 eggs
4 ounces unsweetened baking chocolate, melted and cooled

For frosting:
⅓ cup butter, softened
3 ounces unsweetened baking chocolate, melted and cooled
3 cups confectioners' sugar
½ cup dairy sour cream
2 tsp vanilla

Decadent Choco-Latte Cake

David Schlomer, Kansas City, Missouri

3 ounces unsweetened chocolate
8 tbsp (1 stick) sweet butter
1 cup boiling water
1 tsp vanilla extract
2 cups sugar
2 eggs, separated
1 tsp baking soda
½ cup dairy sour cream
2 cups less 2 tbsp unbleached,
    all-purpose flour, sifted
1 tsp baking powder
2 tbsp instant espresso coffee

For Choco-Latte Frosting:
2 tbsp sweet butter
¾ cup semisweet chocolate chips
6 tbsp heavy cream
1¼ cups sifted confectioners' sugar,
    or more as needed
1 tsp vanilla extract
1 tsp instant espresso coffee

"I try to make things as healthy as possible most of the time," David says. **"But sometimes, you have got to pull out all the stops."**

1. Preheat oven to 350 degrees. Grease and flour a 10-inch tube pan, shaking out excess flour.

2. Place chocolate and butter in a medium bowl, pour boiling water over them and let stand until melted. Stir in vanilla and sugar, then whisk in egg yolks, one at a time, blending well.

3. Mix together baking soda and sour cream, and whisk into the chocolate mixture.

4. Sift together flour, baking powder and instant espresso, and add to the batter, mixing thoroughly.

5. Beat egg whites until stiff, but not dry. Stir a quarter of the egg whites thoroughly into the batter. Scoop remaining egg whites on top of the batter, and gently fold in. Pour the batter into prepared pan.

6. Set on middle rack of oven, and bake 40 to 50 minutes, or until the edges have pulled away from the sides of the pan, and a cake tester inserted into the center comes out clean. Cool in pan on wire rack 10 minutes; remove from pan and cool completely before frosting with Choco-Latte Frosting.

7. For frosting: Place all frosting ingredients in a heavy saucepan over low heat. Whisk until butter and chips are melted, and mixture is smooth. Cool slightly; stir in more sugar if necessary to achieve desired frosting consistency.

Makes 12 servings

Sauerkraut-Cocoa Cake

Mary Gandy, Kansas City, Kansas

Mary culled this recipe years ago from a women's magazine. It wins raves, especially if they can figure out it contains sauerkraut. "When you eat it, you think it's coconut," Mary says.

1. Cream butter with sugar until light and fluffy. Beat in eggs and vanilla.

2. Sift together cocoa, flour, baking powder, baking soda and salt. Add dry mixture alternately with portions of the water, beating after each addition until smooth. Stir in sauerkraut.

3. Spread mixture into 2 greased-and-floured 9-inch square or round cake pans (as an option, use nonstick cooking spray on pans); bake in preheated oven at 350 degrees 30 minutes, or until toothpick inserted in center comes out clean.

4. Cool in pans about 5 minutes, then remove cakes to plates, cover and cool completely. Fill and frost with Sour Cream Chocolate Frosting (see recipe on page 155).

Makes 12 servings

⅔ cup butter or margarine, softened
1½ cups sugar
3 eggs
1 tsp vanilla
½ cup cocoa
2¼ cups sifted all-purpose flour
1 tsp baking powder
1 tsp baking soda
¼ tsp salt
1 cup water
⅔ cup chopped, drained and rinsed
    canned sauerkraut

Blackberry Jam Cake

Mary Alice Broome, Kansas City, Missouri, and Judy Broome, Grain Valley, Missouri

1 cup (2 sticks) butter
2 cups sugar
5 eggs, beaten
2 tsp cinnamon
1 tsp nutmeg
2 tbsp allspice
⅛ tsp salt
1½ tsp baking soda
½ cup cold water
1 cup buttermilk
1 (6 oz) bottle maraschino cherries,
    chopped, reserving liquid
5 cups sifted all-purpose flour
1 cup nuts, chopped and roasted at
    275 degrees until slightly toasted
1 cup raisins
1 cup citron
1 cup currants
1½ cups blackberry jam
Red wine or fruit juice

This heavy, rich cake is akin to a fruit cake. But plan ahead; it requires weeks of infusing with wine before it is ready to serve.

1. Cream butter and sugar. Add eggs, cinnamon, nutmeg, allspice and salt. Mix well.

2. In separate bowl, dissolve baking soda in water; add buttermilk and reserved juice from maraschino cherries.

3. Resift flour and add to creamed mixture alternately with water-buttermilk mixture.

4. Stir in cherries, nuts, raisins, citron, currants and jam. Grease and flour 10-inch Bundt pan and 9- by 5- by 3-inch loaf pan.

5. Divide batter equally between pans. Bake at 275 degrees 2 hours, or until a toothpick inserted in center comes out clean. Cool 15 minutes in pans then invert onto rack and cool completely.

6. Wrap in clean towel or cheesecloth. Saturate cloth with wine or juice. Wrap with plastic wrap and refrigerate. About once every week or 10 days, add more wine to the fabric, wrap and return to the refrigerator. Continue 1 month to 6 weeks.

7. Slice and serve for special occasions, such as Thanksgiving.

Makes about 24 servings

Red Velvet Cake

Bruce and Kathleen Fearon, Lee's Summit, Missouri

This recipe has a long heritage tracing back to Kathleen's great-great-grandmother. Kathleen's great-grandmother added the Nestle Quik. The Fearons describe the cake as extremely rich.

1. Combine strawberry mix and food coloring; set aside.

2. Cream sugar, butter, salt and vanilla until fluffy. Beat in eggs. Add food coloring mixture.

3. Add buttermilk and cake flour; mix well.

4. In a cup, dissolve baking soda in vinegar; add to batter and beat well. Pour into 9-inch round cake pans that have been greased and lined with parchment or wax paper.

5. Bake in at 350 degrees 30 to 35 minutes, or until toothpick inserted in center comes out clean. Do not overcook.

6. Remove cake from pans and cool on wire rack. This is a very dense cake. Frost cake.

7. For frosting: Place flour in top of double boiler over medium heat. Gradually mix milk with flour. Cook, stirring constantly, until thick, about 10 to 12 minutes. Remove from heat and let cool.

8. In a bowl, beat butter and sugar until smooth. Add vanilla and rum extract, and blend. Spoon mixture into cooled milk mixture. Using an electric mixer, beat on high 7 to 10 minutes, or until fluffy and light.

Variation: Substitute chocolate, strawberry, cherry or almond flavoring for rum extract.

Makes 12 to 16 servings

For cake:
3 tbsp instant strawberry milk flavoring mix, such as Nestle Quik
2 ounces red food coloring
1½ cups sugar
1 cup (2 sticks) butter, softened
¼ tsp salt
1 tsp vanilla
2 eggs
1 cup buttermilk
2½ cups cake flour, sifted
1 tsp baking soda
1 tbsp vinegar

For frosting:
3 tbsp all-purpose flour, sifted
1 cup milk
1 cup (2 sticks) butter, softened
1 cup sugar
½ tsp vanilla
½ tsp rum extract

Crumb Cake

Paulette Giarratana, Leawood, Kansas

For cake:
¼ cup (½ stick) butter or margarine, softened
½ cup sugar
1 egg
½ tsp vanilla
1½ cups all-purpose flour
2¹¹/₂ tsp baking powder
¼ tsp salt
½ cup milk

For topping:
1 cup all-purpose flour
1 tbsp cinnamon
3 tbsp sugar
3 tbsp brown sugar
½ cup (1 stick) butter or margarine, slightly softened
Confectioners' sugar

Paulette remembers the childhood thrill of picking sweet morsels form the top of her Aunt Di Di's crumb cake.

1. Preheat oven to 350 degrees.

2. Prepare cake: Cream butter with electric mixer. Add sugar, and beat well. Add egg and vanilla; mix well.

3. Sift together flour, baking powder and salt. Add sifted dry ingredients to creamed mixture alternately with milk. Mix until well combined.

4. Pour batter into a greased 8-inch square pan.

5. Prepare topping: Combine flour, cinnamon, sugar, brown sugar and butter; mix with fingers or pastry blender until well blended. Mixture will be crumbly. Use your fingers to press together portions of the topping to make large and small "crumb" bits.

5. Top cake batter with crumb bits.

6. Bake 30 to 40 minutes, or until toothpick inserted in center comes out clean. Cool completely. Sprinkle with confectioners' sugar before serving.

Note: This recipe makes a good coffee cake or brunch dish. It can be doubled and placed in a 9- by 13-inch pan. Bake as usual.

Makes 9 servings

German Apple Cake

Linda Russell, Merriam, Kansas

1. For cake: Beat eggs, oil and vanilla until foamy. Add sugar, flour, cinnamon, baking soda and salt; blend well. Stir in apples and nuts. Grease and flour a 9- by 13-inch baking pan. Pour batter into pan.

2. Bake at 300 degrees 1 hour, or until crusty on top. Toothpick inserted in center should come out clean.

3. For frosting: Blend cream cheese, butter and vanilla. Gradually add confectioners' sugar, and beat until smooth (it should be spreading consistency). Cake may be frosted warm or after it has cooled.

Note: This cake freezes well.

Makes 12 servings

For cake:
3 eggs
1 cup vegetable oil
1 tsp vanilla
2 cups sugar
2 cups all-purpose flour
2 tsp cinnamon
1 tsp baking soda
½ tsp salt
4 cups thinly sliced, peeled apples (about 4 medium to large apples)
1 cup walnuts, chopped

For frosting:
8 ounces cream cheese, at room temperature
3 tbsp butter, melted
1 tsp vanilla
1½ cups confectioner's sugar

Fruit Desserts

Fruit Cobblers

Judy Baird, Edgerton, Kansas

1 cup all-purpose flour
1 cup sugar
½ tsp salt
1 egg
4 tbsp butter, softened
Fruit filling

One thing Judy especially liked about her cooking is that most of her recipes came from friends and family. "Every time I pull one out, there is a memory attached to it," she said.

1. Stir together flour, sugar, salt, egg and butter until crumbly for topping. If desired, use pastry blender to blend in butter. Set aside.

2. Prepare fruit according to instructions that follow, and spoon into buttered 7½- by 11¾-inch baking dish. Distribute topping over fruit.

3. Bake at 350 degrees oven 45 minutes, or until fruit is tender and topping is lightly browned.

For Peach Cobbler: In large saucepan, stir together 1½ tablespoons cornstarch, ¼ teaspoon ground cinnamon, ½ cup brown sugar and ½ cup water. Bring to a boil over medium-high heat; add 1 tablespoon lemon juice, 1 tablespoon butter and 4 cups peeled, sliced peaches. Gently stir until peach slices are well coated with sugar mixture.

For Apple Cobbler: In large saucepan, combine 1 cup sugar, 2 tablespoons all-purpose flour, ½ teaspoon ground cinnamon and ¼ teaspoon ground nutmeg. Add 6 cups peeled, sliced apples, stirring gently to coat with sugar mixture. Cook over medium heat 7 minutes, or until just slightly softened.

For Cherry Cobbler: Combine 2½ cups tart cherries or 1 (20 oz) drained can tart cherries, ½ cup sugar, 1 tablespoon cooking tapioca and 1 tablespoon butter. Stir until well blended.

Makes 8 to 10 servings

Apple Crisp

Arleta and Dick Johnson, Kansas City, Missouri, now retired to Texas

Arleta likes to prepare desserts and meals for guests and for holidays, while Dick is interested in main courses, vegetables and everyday cooking.

1. Place sliced apples in 9-inch-square baking dish treated with nonstick cooking spray.

2. Mix together well brown sugar, flour, oatmeal, nutmeg, cinnamon, sesame seeds and nuts. Add melted margarine, and stir. Sprinkle over apples.

3. Bake at 375 degrees 30 minutes, or until apples are tender and topping is browned.

Makes 6 to 8 servings

5 to 6 apples, sliced
⅔ cup brown sugar
⅓ cup all-purpose flour
⅔ cup oatmeal
½ tsp nutmeg
¾ tsp cinnamon
2 tbsp sesame seeds
1 cup chopped nuts
⅓ cup melted margarine

Kansas Rhubarb

Sondra O'Connor, Plattsburg, Missouri

6 cups diced rhubarb
3½ cups sugar, divided
6 tbsp butter, softened
2 cups all-purpose flour
2 tsp baking powder
1 tsp salt, divided
1 cup milk
2 tbsp cornstarch
¾ cup boiling water

This dessert forms its own unusual crust.

1. Spread rhubarb over bottom of 9- by 13-inch baking pan. In a mixing bowl, cream together 1½ cups sugar and butter.

2. Into another bowl, sift flour, baking powder and ½ teaspoon salt. Add portions of flour mixture to sugar mixture, alternating with portions of milk; mix well. Spread mixture over rhubarb.

3. Mix remaining 2 cups sugar, cornstarch and remaining ½ teaspoon salt. Sprinkle over batter.

4. Slowly pour or spoon boiling water over the top. Bake at 350 degrees 1 hour. The top will look crusty, uneven and a light golden brown.

Variations: Substitute fresh peeled and sliced peaches or apples for the rhubarb.

Makes 8 to 10 servings

Persimmon Pudding

Kathy and Steve Peters, Kansas City, Kansas

Kathy and Steve save fruit from their persimmon tree to make this rich dessert.

1. Preheat oven to 350 degrees. Place butter in 9- by 13- by 2-inch baking dish; place dish in oven as oven is heating to melt butter and grease dish.

2. Beat eggs in large mixing bowl. One by one, add persimmon pulp, sugar, brown sugar and melted butter, stirring well after each addition.

3. Combine and sift baking soda, salt, baking powder, nutmeg, cinnamon, ginger and flour. Add to persimmon mixture; stir. Stir in whipping cream then chopped nuts, mixing well.

4. Pour mixture into prepared dish. Bake about 1 hour, or until toothpick or knife inserted in center comes out clean.

Notes: You may substitute milk or half-and-half for the cream. You also can vary slightly the amount of persimmon pulp, according to what you have available.

Makes about 24 servings

½ cup (1 stick) butter
3 eggs
1¾ cups persimmon pulp
¾ cup sugar
½ cup brown sugar
1 tsp baking soda
½ tsp salt
1 tsp baking powder
1 tsp nutmeg
1 tsp cinnamon
½ tsp ground ginger
1 cup all-purpose flour
1 cup whipping cream
1 cup chopped nuts

Cranberry Torte

Shirley Schnug, Overland Park, Kansas

2 cups sugar, divided
2¼ cups all-purpose flour
1 tsp baking soda
1 tsp baking powder
¼ tsp salt
2 eggs, beaten
¾ cup vegetable oil
1 cup buttermilk
2 tsp grated orange rind
1 cup dates, chopped
2 cups whole cranberries
1 cup walnuts or pecans, coarsely
   chopped
1 cup fresh orange juice

Shirley says this dessert can be made ahead of time. In fact, it is best if made ahead. "It has to mellow," she says. "I never have a holiday meal without this dessert; it's a favorite."

1. Combine 1 cup sugar, flour, baking soda, baking powder and salt in large bowl. Add eggs, oil, buttermilk and orange rind. Blend well, then stir in dates, cranberries and nuts.

2. Pour into greased 10-inch springform or false-bottom pan with 4-inch center ring. (You can try a tube pan, but the cake can be difficult to unmold because dates often stick.)

3. Bake at 350 degrees 1 hour, or until toothpick inserted in center comes out clean and torte pulls away slightly from side of pan. Allow torte to cool 5 to 10 minutes, until cool enough to handle. Run knife around edge of torte and remove from pan before inverting torte, right side up, onto serving plate.

4. While torte bakes, cook together orange juice and remaining 1 cup sugar over high heat until sugar is dissolved, about 3 minutes. Pour juice mixture over torte as soon as it is on serving plate. Torte is best if made 2 to 3 days before serving. Keep refrigerated.

Makes 16 to 20 servings

Fruit Torte

Alan Edelman and Debbie Sosland-Edelman, Leawood, Kansas

This dish was inspired by the Jewish holiday of Sukkot, which is celebrated in the fall. "Alan and I like to use the time to entertain," says Debbie.

1. Cream together butter and sugar, beat in eggs and gradually add flour and baking powder.

2. Spoon mixture into a greased 9- or 10-inch springform pan. Top with sliced fruit, placed in a single layer with edges overlapping. Arranging slices in concentric circles makes an attractive presentation. Sprinkle with cinnamon sugar.

3. Bake at 350 degrees 1 hour, or until fruit is tender and crust is golden. Cool, remove ring and serve.

Note: To make cinnamon sugar, combine ¼ cup sugar with ½ teaspoon cinnamon.

Makes 6 to 8 servings

½ cup (1 stick) butter or margarine
1 cup sugar
2 eggs
1 cup all-purpose flour
1 tsp baking powder
Sliced fresh fruit (about 4 medium pears, peaches, plums or apples)
¼ cup cinnamon sugar, or to taste (see note)

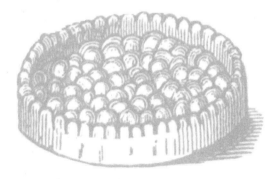

Pies & Pastries

Anna Lee's Banana Cream Pie

Ann Amos, Kansas City, Missouri

½ cup sugar
⅓ tsp salt
2 tbsp cornstarch
¾ tbsp all-purpose flour
2¼ cups whole milk
2 eggs, beaten
¾ tbsp butter
1 tsp vanilla extract
1 cup sliced banana
1 (9-inch) baked pie shell

For topping:
½ cup whipping cream
¼ tsp vanilla extract
1 to 2 tbsp sugar, to taste

"The main thing I like to do is bake pies, and I do bake good ones," Ann says with a laugh. "I take them to church. I always take pies, and they're always gone."

1. In a large saucepan or double boiler combine ½ cup sugar, salt, cornstarch and flour.

2. Gradually add milk and eggs, stirring constantly, over medium-low heat. Cook and stir until mixture thickens, 15 to 20 minutes.

3. Remove pan from heat and strain mixture into large bowl to remove any lumps. Stir in butter and 1 teaspoon vanilla. Cool to room temperature.

4. When filling is completely cooled, gently fold in sliced bananas, and pour into baked pie shell. Refrigerate until ready to serve.

5. Prepare topping by whipping cream with ¼ teaspoon vanilla and 1 to 2 tablespoons sugar until stiff peaks form. Spread on top of pie and serve immediately.

Variations: Substitute drained, crushed pineapple or coconut for the bananas.

Makes 6 to 8 servings

Raquel's Capirotada (Mexican Bread Pudding)

Carlos and Teresa Pacheco, Kansas City, Kansas

1. Butter a large casserole (9¾-inch square or 9- by 13-inch) that has an ovenproof cover.

2. Cut bread into ¾-inch slices. Toast at 400 degrees until golden; cool.

3. Make syrup: In a large, heavy Dutch oven, add water, brown sugar, sugar, piloncillo, cinnamon, cloves, onion, tomato, chile ancho and salt; stir. Bring to a rapid boil, lower heat and keep stirring. Simmer 1½ to 2 hours, stirring occasionally, until syrup forms.

4. Place about ⅓ toasted bread on bottom of casserole dish. Pour syrup over until bread is well coated. Sprinkle with scant ½ cup cheese and raisins, and a scant ¼ cup nuts. Repeat layers twice. The capirotada should be moist. Bake at 375 degrees 20 minutes, or until heated through. Serve warm or cold.

Note: Piloncillo, chili ancho and queso manchego are available in Mexican specialty food stores, or supermarkets will special order.

Makes 8 servings

1 loaf French bread
6 cups cold water
2½ cups brown sugar
1 cup sugar
6 cubes piloncillo, or substitute with additional ½ cup brown sugar
3 sticks cinnamon
12 whole cloves
⅛ medium onion
½ fresh medium tomato
½ piece of whole chili ancho (without seeds)
½ tsp salt
1 cup shredded cheese (queso manchego, Muenster, longhorn, mild cheddar)
1 cup raisins
½ cup slivered almonds or pecans

Miniature Nut-Filled Pastries

Kay Gray, Lee's Summit, Missouri

2½ cups all-purpose flour
1 cup butter, cut in pieces
2 egg yolks, slightly beaten
½ cup dairy sour cream
2 cups finely chopped nuts
⅔ cup dark corn syrup
Confectioners' sugar

"Wherever we have lived, I always checked out recipes and met neighbors—in Germany, all over Europe, Japan, Okinawa and many parts of the United States," says Kay. These miniature pastries are the sort found in many Middle European countries.

1. Put flour and butter in large bowl. Using pastry blender or two knives, cut in butter until the size of peas. Stir in egg yolks and sour cream until well mixed.

2. Turn onto floured surface and knead until smooth, about 1 to 2 minutes. Wrap dough in plastic and chill 20 minutes.

3. Stir nuts and corn syrup together and set aside for filling.

4. Divide dough into 4 equal pieces. Roll each piece into a rectangle ⅛-inch thick. Cut rectangle into 2-inch squares. A crimped cutter looks best.

5. Put ½ teaspoon nut filling diagonally across each square. Dampen one corner of square with a little water, and bring up the corners to meet in the center of the filling. Pinch the corners together firmly to secure.

6. Bake about 1 inch apart on an ungreased baking sheet at 400 degrees 12 minutes, or until edges are lightly brown. Cool completely before sprinkling with confectioners' sugar.

Tips: To avoid adding flour while rolling out dough, sprinkle counter with water. Place large strip of heavy plastic wrap over water, which will hold plastic to counter. Place dough on plastic, flatten, and place another plastic sheet on top. This process eliminates the need to add flour and thus keeps dough its most tender.

For easier assembly, place dough squares about ½ inch apart on baking sheet before filling. Once filled and sealed, they are ready to bake.

Makes 3 to 3½ dozen cookies

Vinegar Pie

Alma Marshall, Kansas City, Missouri

Alma enjoys baking, and her old-fashioned vinegar pie is a favorite. "It's something different. People say, 'Vinegar pie! Are you crazy? Who wants vinegar pie?' " Those who've tasted it, though, know better.

1. Cream together butter and sugar. Add eggs one at a time, beating well after each addition. Add vinegar and vanilla; mix well. Pour mixture into 3 (9-inch) pie shells.

2. Bake at 350 degrees 45 minutes, or until brown and firm.

Makes 3 (9-inch) pies

1 cup (2 sticks) butter, softened
3 cups sugar
9 eggs
¾ cup white vinegar
1 tsp vanilla
3 unbaked 9-inch pie shells

Plum and Apricot Marzipan Tart

Virginia and Gary Jensen, Kansas City, Missouri

1¼ cups all-purpose flour
⅛ tsp salt
5 tbsp cold unsalted butter, cut into pieces, and 2 tbsp melted butter
1 egg, lightly beaten
1 (7 oz) package marzipan or almond paste
¾ pound (6 to 7) small red plums, cut in half lengthwise and pitted
½ pound (3 to 4) apricots, cut in half lengthwise and pitted
1 to 2 tbsp sugar, optional, according to taste

Gary describes Virginia as a gourmet cook and says he is her assistant. Virginia gives the credit to cooking classes and mountains of cookbooks and cooking magazines.

1. Preheat oven to 400 degrees. Butter a 9½- by 1-inch false-bottom tart pan.

2. In medium bowl, combine flour and salt. Rub or cut cold butter into flour mixture until it resembles fine bread crumbs.

3. Stir in egg; gather dough into a smooth ball. On a lightly floured surface, roll dough into an 11-inch circle. Line prepared pan with dough, trying not to stretch dough. Trim pastry level with rim of pan by gently rolling a pin across the top.

4. Roll marzipan into a ball. On lightly floured surface, roll marzipan into a 9-inch circle. Gently press marzipan circle onto dough in pan.

5. Cut each plum and apricot half into 3 lengthwise pieces. Arrange wedges in pan, skin-side down, in alternating concentric circles, starting with plums at outer edge. At this point, tart can be covered and refrigerated up to 12 hours before baking.

6. Brush fruit with melted butter. If fruit is tart, sprinkle with optional sugar. Set tart on a baking sheet and bake in middle of oven until fruit is tender and pastry is crisp and nicely browned, about 45 minutes.

7. Place on rack to cool to room temperature. Unmold onto flat platter before serving.

Adapted from *The Best of Food & Wine 1989 Collection.*

Makes 6 to 8 servings

Strawberry Pie

Mike and Carolyn Esberg, Kansas City, Missouri

1. Preheat oven to 350 degrees. To prepare crust, grind crumbs and walnuts in food processor until coarse crumb texture. Add melted butter and mix with hands. Press over bottom and sides of a 9-inch pie pan.

2. Bake 6 to 8 minutes, or until browned slightly. Set aside to cool.

3. Crush 1 pint strawberries in 1-quart saucepan. Add water, sugar and cornstarch, and cook, stirring frequently, over medium-low heat until mixture boils and is clear and thickened, about 10 to 15 minutes. Let stand until cool enough to touch. Stir in the lemon juice.

4. Arrange remaining pint of whole, hulled strawberries in cooked graham cracker shell, pointed ends of strawberries up. Pour cooled strawberry filling over whole berries. Refrigerate 2 to 3 hours, or until filling is set.

5. Serve garnished with whipped cream and whole strawberries.

Adapted from *California Fresh* cookbook.

Makes 6 to 8 servings

1 cup graham cracker crumbs (about 18 single cracker squares)
½ cup sliced walnuts
5 tbsp butter, melted
2 pints whole strawberries, washed and hulled, divided
½ cup water
1 cup sugar
2½ tbsp cornstarch
Juice of ½ lemon
Whipped cream, for garnish
8 whole strawberries, for garnish

Strawberry–Cream Cheese Pie

Louise Feeney, Independence, Missouri

1 cup sugar
3 tbsp cornstarch
2 pints fresh strawberries, washed
    and hulled, divided
3 tbsp strawberry gelatin
4 ounces cream cheese, softened
1 (9-inch) baked pie shell
Whipped cream, for garnish

Louise likes variety, but she thinks pie-making may be her best cooking skill. One of her favorite recipes is strawberry pie.

1. Mix together sugar and cornstarch; set aside.

2. Crush (don't puree) 1 pint strawberries in blender or with potato masher, and add enough water to make 1½ cups. Place in saucepan, and bring to boil over medium heat.

3. Stir in sugar and cornstarch all at one time. Stir constantly until thick and clear. Remove from heat, and add strawberry gelatin. Stir until gelatin is dissolved. Set aside.

4. Mix cream cheese and 1 tablespoon hot cooked strawberries; spread mixture over baked pastry shell.

5. Stand remaining pint uncooked whole strawberries, stem end down, on top of cream cheese. Pour hot cooked strawberries over raw strawberries. Refrigerate until set, about 3 hours. Cover with whipped cream and serve.

Makes 6 to 8 servings

Soda Cracker Torte

Mary Zimmerman, Prairie Village, Kansas

Here is a dessert that is eye-catching and delicious but takes just minutes to prepare. "It's something I make if I have company coming at the last minute, or if I want a stunning dessert but don't have time to put into because I've spent so much time on the main courses," Mary says.

1. Combine crackers, sugar, baking powder and nuts.

2. Blend vanilla into egg whites; fold mixture into dry ingredients.

3. Smooth mixture into buttered 9-inch pie pan or 8- or 9-inch cake pan. Bake at 350 degrees 30 minutes, or until lightly brown.

4. Cool, and top with your choice of sliced fruit or berries along with whipped cream. Ice cream also can be used as garnish.

Note: Adding a little liqueur, such as Amaretto, to the whipped cream makes this dessert even more elegant.

Makes 6 servings

12 individual saltine crackers, rolled fine
1 cup sugar
1 tsp baking powder
3/4 cup chopped pecans or walnuts
1 tsp vanilla
3 egg whites, beaten very stiff
Sliced fruit or berries
Whipped cream

Chocolate Cheesecake

Stephanie McCorkle, Kansas City, Missouri

For crust:
1 (8½ oz) package chocolate wafers,
    crushed
6 tbsp butter, melted

For filling:
16 ounces cream cheese, softened
⅔ cup sugar
3 eggs
12 ounces semisweet chocolate
    chips, melted
1 cup whipping cream
2 tbsp butter, melted
1 tsp vanilla

For topping:
1 cup dairy sour cream
1 tsp sugar
½ tsp vanilla
½ ounce unsweetened chocolate
½ tsp shortening

Stephanie always wraps her springform pans in foil to prevent them from leaking and sets them in a second pan with ½ inch or so of water. Voilà! No cracks.

1. For crust: In medium bowl, combine crushed wafers and 6 tablespoons melted butter. Press over bottom and 2 inches up sides of 9-inch springform pan. Refrigerate.

2. For filling: In large bowl, mix cream cheese and ⅔ cup sugar; beat until smooth. Add eggs, one at a time, beating well after each addition until well blended. Add melted semisweet chocolate; beat well.

3. Add whipping cream, 2 tablespoons melted butter and 1 teaspoon vanilla; beat until smooth. Pour into crust-lined pan.

4. Bake at 325 degrees 55 to 60 minutes, or until edges are set (center of cheesecake will be soft). Cool in pan 5 minutes; remove sides of pan. Cool. Refrigerate overnight.

5. For topping: Blend together sour cream, 1 teaspoon sugar and ½ teaspoon vanilla. Spread over cooled cheesecake. Melt unsweetened chocolate and shortening in small pan over low heat. Drizzle over sour cream topping, and serve.

Makes 16 servings

Passover Streusel-Top and Nut Cheesecake

Rabbi Gerald Kane and Cyrille Kane, Leawood, Kansas

Gerald and Cyrille, avid cooks, developed their Passover cheesecake for an event in Phoenix.

1. Preheat oven to 350 degrees.

2. Make crust: Mix together all crust ingredients; blend well. Press into bottom and up sides of a greased 8-inch square pan or a 9-inch springform pan. Bake 5 to 7 minutes, or until set. Remove from oven and allow to cool.

3. Make filling: In bowl of food processor fitted with steel blade, blend together cream cheese and sugar. Add eggs one at a time and blend after each addition. Add sour cream, lemon rind and vanilla; blend. Scrape sides of bowl and mix well. Pour over cooled crust.

4. Make topping: In small bowl, combine all topping ingredients. Mix with fingers until crumbly. Sprinkle evenly over cheese filling.

5. Bake in the middle of oven at 350 degrees 45 to 55 minutes, until set. Cool on a rack to room temperature. Cover and refrigerate 8 hours or overnight.

6. Remove from refrigerator about 10 minutes before serving. Removing ring or serving from square pan will be easier if you first run warm spatula blade around inside edge of pan.

Makes 10 to 12 servings

For crust:
2 cups finely chopped pecans
1 cup shredded coconut, optional
3 tbsp sugar
1 tsp cinnamon
¼ tsp ground ginger
6 tbsp melted butter or margarine

For filling:
16 ounces cream cheese
¾ cup sugar
3 large eggs
½ cup dairy sour cream
1 tsp freshly grated lemon rind
1 tsp vanilla extract

For topping:
¼ cup firmly packed brown sugar
2 tbsp potato starch (all-purpose flour will work fine if not for Passover)
1 tbsp butter or margarine
½ tsp cinnamon
½ cup finely chopped almonds
½ cup coarsely chopped Passover semisweet chocolate; if not for Passover you may substitute equivalent amount of semisweet chocolate chips

Brownie Parfait

Debby Bjerkan, Leawood, Kansas

1 (15.5 oz) box brownie mix, prepared, baked and cooled

1½ cups, approximately, of your choice of sliced fresh strawberries, fresh blueberries, cherry pie filling, blueberry pie filling or caramel sauce and peanuts

1 (16 oz) container frozen nondairy whipped topping

16 ounces chocolate syrup

1½ cups toffee chips, such as Skor (generally found next to chocolate chips in markets)

1. In a trifle bowl or other fun bowl (about 2 quarts), layer ⅓ of the brownies, crumbled; ½ cup of strawberries, blueberries, pie filling, or caramel sauce and peanuts; ⅓ whipped topping, ⅓ chocolate syrup and ⅓ toffee chips.

2. Repeat layers twice.

3. Cover and refrigerate overnight. Spoon into dessert bowls to serve.

Makes 8 to 12 servings

Sour Cream Chocolate Frosting

Mary Gandy, Kansas City, Kansas

1. Melt chocolate and butter in pan over low heat. Cool thoroughly.

2. In a bowl, mix together sour cream, sugar and salt. Gradually stir in cooled chocolate mixture. Add vanilla. Beat well.

3. Add more powdered sugar as needed to get desired consistency.

Note: Use to frost Sauerkraut-Cocoa Cake.

Makes enough for a 2-layer cake.

3 ounces unsweetened chocolate
2 tbsp butter or margarine
¾ cup dairy sour cream
4½ cups sifted confectioners' sugar, or more
¼ tsp salt
1 tsp vanilla

Confectioners' Icing

Mary Lickteig, Overland Park, Kansas

1. Add half-and-half to confectioners' sugar, stirring until mixture reaches spreading consistency. Add vanilla and food coloring, if desired. For variety, divide the white frosting among several small bowls and add different colors to each bowl.

Makes enough for 3 to 4 dozen cookies

About ¼ cup half-and-half, or milk
2 cups sifted confectioners' sugar
1 tsp vanilla
Food coloring, optional

Mom D's White Frosting

Kathy Dickinson, Kansas City, Missouri

¼ cup all-purpose flour
1 cup milk
½ cup (1 stick) margarine
½ cup shortening
1 cup sugar
1 tsp vanilla

Kathy says this unusual frosting is light and versatile. "It stays soft and doesn't set. I make a double batch and freeze half. The next time I make a cake, I pull it out of the freezer, and it's ready to use by the time the cake cools," Kathy says.

1. In small saucepan, make a paste with the flour and a little of the milk. Gradually add remaining milk, stirring constantly to avoid lumps. Cook over medium heat, stirring constantly, until mixture forms a thick, white sauce. Cool to room temperature.

2. In a large bowl, beat margarine and shortening with electric mixer until light and fluffy. Very gradually add sugar, beating on high speed until mixture no longer feels grainy.

3. Beat in milk-flour mixture and vanilla, and frost cake or cupcakes.

4. Store frosted cake in refrigerator. Leftover frosting can be frozen for later use. Simply thaw and spread.

Makes enough to frost 2 cake layers

The Breadbasket
Quick Breads, Yeast Breads

Quick Breads

Oat Bran Muffins

Angela Candela, Lawrence, Kansas

3 cups oat bran
1½ cups whole-wheat flour
¾ cup sugar
1 tsp salt
1 tbsp cinnamon
2 tbsp baking powder
2 apples, diced
2 cups milk
¼ cup canola oil or vegetable oil
2 ripe bananas
4 egg whites

1. Preheat oven to 425 degrees. In large bowl, mix together oat bran, flour, sugar, salt, cinnamon, baking powder and apples.

2. In blender, blend milk, oil, bananas and egg whites until smooth; pour into dry ingredients. Stir until dry ingredients are well moistened.

3. Fill paper-lined muffin cups ⅔ full.

4. Bake 17 to 20 minutes, or until lightly browned and tops spring back when pressed with finger. These muffins freeze well.

Variations: Instead of apples and cinnamon, substitute 1½ cups raspberries, diced peaches or diced pineapple; 1½ cups blueberries, zest from 1 lemon and 1 tablespoon cinnamon; 1½ cups diced pears and 1½ teaspoons ground ginger; 1½ cups grated carrot or zucchini plus ½ cup raisins and ¼ teaspoons nutmeg, ⅛ teaspoon cloves, ⅛ teaspoon allspice and 1½ teaspoons cinnamon. Try topping muffins with a sprinkling of brown sugar or a nut half.

Makes 2 dozen

Banana and Carrot Muffins

Mary Libeer, Gladstone, Missouri

"I try to do recipes with some flexibility. I try to emphasize you can improvise, and with some creativity and imagination, you can come up with something (new)," Mary says. That's how Mary developed this muffin recipe, with a little imagination and some bananas she needed to use.

1. Cream margarine and sugar. Mix about 3 minutes. Add remaining ingredients and mix well.

2. Grease mini-muffin tins or standard muffin tins, or treat tins with nonstick cooking spray. Fill cups about half full.

3. Bake at 350 degrees 12 to 15 minutes for mini-muffins, 20 to 25 minutes for standard muffins, or until center springs back when touched lightly. Remove from pan and cool on cooling rack.

Makes about 1½ dozen standard muffins

⅔ cup margarine, softened
1½ cups sugar
3 eggs
2 tsp baking soda
1½ cups mashed bananas
1 tsp vanilla
½ cup sour milk
1 cup chopped nuts, optional
½ tsp salt
1 tsp baking powder
1 tsp cinnamon
1 cup grated carrots
2½ cups all-purpose flour

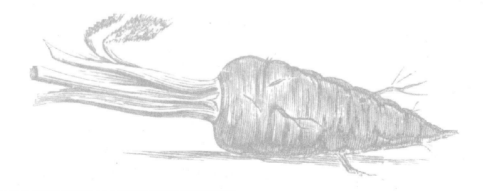

Mollie's Irish Soda Bread

Peggy Sheehan, Roeland Park, Kansas

2 cups all-purpose flour
1 tsp baking powder
1 tsp baking soda
½ tsp salt
3 tbsp sugar
2 eggs, beaten
2 tbsp cooking oil
1 cup buttermilk
½ cup raisins, soaked overnight in
  water

1. Sift flour, baking powder, baking soda and salt in a large bowl. Stir in remaining ingredients, forming a loose dough.

2. Turn onto a lightly floured board and knead lightly until the top of bread is smooth and a circle is formed. (It is important that dough not be overworked, otherwise it will become tough.)

3. Slash a cross on top with a sharp knife. Place on a lightly floured baking sheet, and bake at 350 degrees 40 to 50 minutes, or until bread sounds hollow when tapped with finger. Cool on rack.

Makes 1 loaf

Refrigerated Muffins

Charlene Blackwell, Gladstone, Missouri

1 (15 oz) box raisin bran cereal
3 cups sugar
5 cups all-purpose flour
2 tsp salt
5 tsp baking soda
4 eggs, beaten
1 cup melted shortening
1 quart buttermilk

1. Mix cereal, sugar, flour, salt and baking soda in large mixing bowl. Add eggs, shortening and buttermilk. Mix well.

2. Cover and store in refrigerator, or bake immediately. Use batter, which keeps for weeks, as needed.

3. To bake muffins, fill lightly greased muffin tins ¾ full and bake at 400 degrees 15 to 20 minutes, or until toothpick inserted in center comes out clean.

Makes 5 to 6 dozen

Beignets

Rosa Freeman, Kansas City, Missouri

Rosa grew up in Oklahoma, and she learned much of her cooking from her Louisiana-born grandparents. "In the South, you want to be as good a cook as the other women in the family so you don't let anyone down," Rosa says. These beignets are a testament to Rosa's standing as a cook.

1. Sift flour, sugar, baking powder and baking soda into bowl. Add milk and egg, and mix well.

2. Drop by tablespoonfuls into deep fat heated to 375 degrees. Fry until golden, about 30 seconds to 1 minute; watch closely.

3. Drain on paper towels. Serve with syrup and butter.

Makes about 6 servings

2 cups all-purpose flour
1 tbsp sugar
1 tsp baking powder
⅛ tsp baking soda
1 cup milk
1 egg

Rhubarb Bread

Tracy Torres, Kansas City, Missouri

1 cup buttermilk or sour milk
1½ cups packed brown sugar
1 egg
⅔ cup oil
2½ cups all-purpose flour
1 tsp salt
1 tsp baking soda
1 tsp vanilla
1½ cups chopped rhubarb
½ cup chopped nuts
½ cup sugar
1 tbsp butter, softened

Tracy often made this bread for her late father, who loved rhubarb.

1. Mix buttermilk, brown sugar, egg and oil in mixing bowl. Add flour, salt, baking soda and vanilla, and blend.

2. Stir in rhubarb and nuts.

3. Pour into two (9- by 5- by 3-inch) loaf pans that have been greased and lightly floured.

4. Combine sugar and butter, and crumble half over top of each pan.

5. Bake at 350 degrees 60 minutes, or until toothpick inserted in center comes out clean.

Makes 2 loaves

Swedish Rye Bread

Evelyn True, Prairie Village, Kansas

Evelyn grew up in Osage City, Kansas, and her family was Swedish. "Having Swedish rye bread has been in the family as long as I can remember," she says. "You just made it."

1. In saucepan mix together water, 1 tablespoon sugar, brown sugar, molasses, salt and shortening. Heat to lukewarm. Remove from heat and add yeast. Let stand 5 minutes, then pour into mixing bowl.

2. Stir in rye flour and enough white flour to make a soft dough. Knead a few minutes on floured surface. Return to bowl, cover with towel and let rise until double in bulk, about 1 to 1½ hours.

3. Divide into 4 equal parts, and form into loaves. Let rise in greased (7½- by 4- by 3-inch) loaf pans, until double in bulk, about 45 minutes to 1 hour.

4. Bake at 350 degrees 30 minutes, or until brown. Remove from pans and cool on racks.

Note: If you can find it, use regular rye flour, instead of stone-ground rye flour, for finer texture.

Makes 4 loaves

3 cups water
1 tbsp sugar
¼ cup brown sugar
¾ cup molasses
1 tsp salt
2 tbsp shortening
2 envelopes dry yeast
4 cups rye flour
5 to 6 cups white flour

Irish Muffin Bread

Ann Buck Renne, Prairie Village, Kansas

2½ cups milk, divided
2½ cups water, divided
1 envelope active dry yeast
½ cup warm water (about 110 degrees)
2½ tbsp sugar
4 tsp salt
2½ tbsp margarine
4 to 5 pounds all-purpose flour
Melted butter, about 2 tbsp

Ann's grandmother always said a blessing when she made two slashes, in the form of a cross, in the top of the bread: "God bless those who eat this bread, and God bless those who make it."

1. Put 1¼ cups milk and 1¼ cups water in a saucepan and scald.

2. Put yeast in a cup, and add ½ cup warm water to dissolve; stir.

3. Place sugar, salt and margarine in a large bowl. Pour scalded water-and-milk mixture over sugar mixture. Stir; after margarine has melted, add the remaining 1¼ cups milk and remaining 1¼ cups water. Stir in enough flour to make a thin batter, and stir in yeast. (Take the phone off the hook now!)

4. Add enough flour to make dough that can be handled easily on a floured surface. Turn out onto floured surface, and continue working in flour until dough is no longer tacky. Knead a few minutes so that all flour is well incorporated; form into a ball.

5. Turn a greased bowl upside down over ball of dough; let dough rest 10 to 15 minutes. Knead again 10 to 15 minutes, until smooth and elastic and only slightly tacky. (If too tacky, add flour to board.) Place dough in the greased bowl. Turn dough to coat with grease. Cover with a kitchen towel, and let rise until double in bulk, 2 to 3 hours.

6. Knead again; cut into four equal pieces. Knead each until smooth, and form into a loaf shape. Place in greased 9- by 5-inch bread pans.

7. Slash the top with a knife down the center. Brush melted butter on top. Cover again, and allow to rise again until double in size, 2 to 3 hours more.

8. Bake at 350 degrees 1 hour. To test for doneness, slide loaf from pan and thump on bottom; it should have a hollow sound. When loaves are done, immediately turn out of pans onto cooling rack. You may serve bread warm, or toasted with marmalade. May be frozen after cooling.

Notes: Loaves rise a lot when they bake; do not be alarmed if they expand over edge of pan. Dough can be refrigerated and baked later if necessary.

Makes 4 loaves

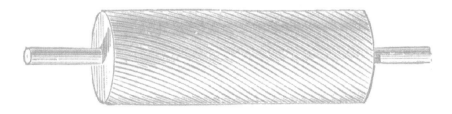

Never-Fail Rolls

Brenda Bell, Kansas City, Missouri

1 cup milk
½ cup margarine
½ cup plus 1 tbsp sugar, divided
2 tsp salt
3 eggs, well-beaten
4½ to 5 cups all-purpose flour, divided
3 (¼ oz) envelopes dry yeast
¼ cup warm water (100 degrees to 120 degrees)

"Mostly, I like dealing with breads," Brenda says. Brenda's homemade rolls are a standard feature at holidays and for other special occasions.

1. Heat milk and margarine together in saucepan until margarine melts. Pour into large mixing bowl to cool 5 to 10 minutes, until lukewarm.

2. Add ½ cup sugar, salt and eggs; mix. Add 2 cups flour to milk mixture, and stir well.

3. Dissolve yeast and 1 tablespoon sugar in water and add to flour mixture. Stir in enough of the remaining flour to make a sticky dough.

4. Turn out onto well-floured surface, and sprinkle well with enough additional flour to make dough easy to handle. Knead 3 to 5 minutes, or until dough feels light.

5. Place dough in greased bowl. Cover and let rise until doubled in bulk, about 1 hour. Punch down; shape dough as desired.

6. Cover and let rise until double, about 45 to 50 minutes.

7. Bake at 375 degrees 15 to 20 minutes, or until lightly brown and rolls sound hollow when tapped with finger.

Variation: To prepare in advance, put dough in greased bowl after first rising and refrigerate overnight. Remove from refrigerator 2 to 3 hours before baking. Shape, let rise, and bake as before. (Rising will take longer, about 2 hours, because dough starts out cold.)

Makes 15 to 20 large rolls or 3 dozen small rolls

Poppy-Swirl Loaves

Sharon Cook, Overland Park, Kansas

The double swirls of black seeds make a striking presentation. This bread is a tasty breakfast or tea bread.

1. In large bowl, mix yeast, water, and 1 teaspoon sugar. Let stand until foamy, 5 to 10 minutes. Add milk, 1/3 cup sugar, 1/4 cup margarine, eggs, yolks, lemon extract and vanilla. Mix well.

2. Beat in salt and 2 to 3 cups flour until dough is soft and thick. Turn out on floured surface. Clean and grease bowl. Knead dough 6 to 8 minutes, using remaining flour to make smooth, elastic dough. Place in bowl, and turn greased side up.

3. Cover and let rise in warm place until double, about 1 hour.

4. While dough is rising, prepare filling: Bring water to boil with poppy seeds. Remove from heat, cover and let sit 30 minutes. Drain water well. Stir in remaining filling ingredients.

5. After dough has risen, punch down and knead 30 seconds to take out the air. Divide in half. Roll dough into 2 (18- by 10-inch) rectangles. Spread each rectangle with half the poppy filling.

6. Beginning on long side of rectangle, roll jelly-roll fashion. With seam side down, fold in half to make a tight "U" shape. Place in greased 9- by 5-inch bread pans.

7. Cover and let rise 45 to 60 minutes, until dough is 1 inch or so over sides of pan.

8. Bake at 350 degrees 35 to 45 minutes, or until golden brown. Brush loaves with melted margarine. Cool in pans about 5 minutes, then cool completely on rack. Slice and toast if you like. This bread freezes well.

2 envelopes active dry yeast
1/3 cup warm water
1/3 cup plus 1 tsp sugar
1 cup milk, at room temperature
1/4 cup melted margarine, plus
    additional for tops of loaves
2 eggs, at room temperature
2 egg yolks, at room temperature
1/4 tsp lemon extract
1 tsp vanilla
1 tsp salt
5 1/2 to 6 cups all-purpose flour

For filling:
1 cup water
3/4 cup poppy seeds
1 cup toasted almonds, chopped
1/4 cup honey
1/3 cup sugar
1/4 tsp salt
3 tbsp half-and-half
1/4 tsp lemon extract
1 tsp vanilla
1/4 tsp almond extract
1 egg white, beaten until stiff

Makes 2 loaves

The Breadbasket

Cream Cheese Braids

Nelda Hoback, Prairie Village, Kansas

1 cup dairy sour cream
½ cup sugar
1 tsp salt
½ cup melted margarine
2 envelopes active dry yeast
½ cup warm water (110 degrees)
2 eggs, beaten
4 cups all-purpose flour

For filling:
16 ounces cream cheese, softened
¾ cup sugar
1 egg, beaten
⅛ tsp salt
2 tsp almond extract

For glaze:
4 tbsp milk
2 cups confectioners' sugar, sifted
2 tsp almond extract

Cream Cheese Braids (which really aren't braided) are great for showers and similar occasions since the recipe makes four coffee cakes.

1. Heat sour cream in saucepan over low heat. Stir in sugar, salt and margarine. Cool to lukewarm.

2. Meanwhile, sprinkle yeast over warm water in large mixing bowl; stir until dissolved. Add cooled sour cream mixture, eggs and flour. Mix well with spoon. Cover tightly and refrigerate overnight.

3. The next day, prepare filling: Cream together cream cheese and sugar. Add egg, salt and almond extract; beat until smooth and creamy.

4. Divide dough into 4 equal parts. Roll out each on a well-floured board into a 12- by 8-inch rectangle. Spread ¼ of filling on each rectangle. Roll up rectangle, starting at long edge and forming a log. Form log into a circle, and pinch ends together to join.

5. Place two circles seam side down on each of two greased baking sheets. Using kitchen shears, cut about ⅔ way through the dough at 2-inch intervals. Cover and let rise in warm place about 1 hour. (Dough will be puffy but won't double in volume.)

6. Bake 12 to 15 minutes at 375 degrees, until lightly browned.

7. Prepare glaze: Gradually stir milk into confectioners' sugar; add almond extract and mix well. Spread over braids while still warm.

8. Serve slightly warm. (Or, cool to room temperature and freeze for later use. Thaw, then warm slightly in microwave oven before serving.)

Note: This delicate pastry complements a breakfast casserole and fruit or juice. Freezes well.

Makes 4 braids, each yielding about 12 slices

Spinning Wheel Whole-Wheat Cinnamon Rolls

Roberta Thompson, Shawnee Mission, Kansas

1 envelope active dry yeast
¼ cup warm water (about 110 degrees)
1 cup (2 sticks) margarine or butter
⅓ cup honey
¾ cup cold milk
2 large eggs
1 tsp salt
4 cups whole-wheat flour
Unbleached all-purpose flour for rolling dough

For filling:
½ cup raisins
½ cup honey
2 tsp cinnamon
¼ cup chopped nuts, optional

Roberta collects recipes, such as this one, when she travels.

1. In small bowl, dissolve yeast in warm water.

2. Melt margarine in microwave in large bowl with tight-fitting lid; add ⅓ cup honey and mix well. Add cold milk to mixture. Stir in eggs, salt, dissolved yeast and whole-wheat flour 1 cup at a time. Stir until well combined. Cover bowl with lid; refrigerate overnight.

3. The next day, take dough out of refrigerator; let sit at room temperature 30 minutes. Work into a ball; turn out on board sprinkled with unbleached all-purpose flour.

4. Sprinkle top of dough with about 1 tablespoon flour to make dough workable. Grease and flour hands; pat dough into a rectangle about 12 inches by 17 inches and ¼-inch thick. This is a wet dough; treat gently.

5. Put raisins in saucepan or small bowl, and cover with very hot tap water; let sit 10 minutes to plump raisins.

6. Spread ½ cup honey on dough; sprinkle with cinnamon.

7. Drain raisins and press between paper towels to dry. Sprinkle raisins and nuts, if desired, over dough.

8. Roll up, starting from long edge; pinch seams together with moistened fingertips. Slice 1-inch rolls with long, light strokes of sharp knife, taking care not to compress dough. Wipe off knife with a damp paper towel between slices.

9. Grease a 9- by 13-inch baking pan and an 8-inch square baking pan. Place cinnamon roll slices about ½ inch apart in pans. Cover; set in warm place to rise until double, about 40 minutes.

10. Bake at 375 degrees 18 to 20 minutes, or until firm to touch. Cool in pans on wire rack.

Makes about 2 dozen

Povtica Bread

Pauline Riga, Platte Woods, Missouri

Her father-in-law tells Pauline that all he wants for Christmas is a loaf of povtica, a rich Polish bread.

3 pounds pecans and English walnuts, finely ground
1 cup (2 sticks) butter, melted
10 eggs, beaten well
4 cups sugar
2 tsp vanilla
3 cups milk, scalded
1 recipe Cinnamon Bread dough (recipe following)

1. Combine pecans, butter, eggs, sugar and vanilla. Stir in milk 1 cup at a time until mixture is thick paste consistency.

2. Roll Cinnamon Bread dough into 3 equal rectangles, as thin as you can make dough without tearing. Spread ⅓ of nut mixture onto each rectangle. Roll dough jelly roll–style.

3. Lay dough in "S" shape in 9- by 5- by 3-inch loaf pan. Bake at 300 degrees 45 minutes; reduce temperature to 200 degrees, and bake 45 minutes more, or until golden brown. A toothpick in the center will come out clean.

4. Remove from pan at once. Place on rack to cool.

Makes 3 loaves

Cinnamon Bread

Pauline Riga, Platte Woods, Missouri

2 cups whole milk
½ cup (1 stick) margarine or butter
⅓ cup honey
1 tsp salt
3 eggs
2 envelopes active dry yeast
6 to 7 cups all-purpose flour, divided

For cinnamon filling:
3 cups sugar
6 tbsp cinnamon
6 tbsp milk or evaporated milk

Pauline rolls out the dough for Cinnamon Bread on tea towels. When it is time to roll the dough over the filling, she simply lifts the edge with the towel. The dough rolls over on itself, making a tricky task easy.

1. Heat milk, margarine, honey and salt in microwave about 2 minutes on high, until margarine is melted and milk is hot. Set aside to cool.

2. Beat 2 of the eggs in large bowl. Add lukewarm milk mixture (115 degrees) to eggs.

3. Mix yeast with 3 cups flour. Stir into egg mixture. Beat well. If preparing in heavy-duty mixer with dough hook, gradually add additional flour until dough pulls away from the sides of the mixing bowl.

    If preparing by hand, stir in flour until dough is too stiff to stir, then work with hands and knead in bowl until dough is soft and pliable. Keep dough soft; you should be able to lift an edge of dough to knead with 1 hand.

4. Grease bowl; place dough in bowl, covered, and let rise in warm place until double in size, about 1 hour.

5. Combine sugar and cinnamon.

6. After dough has doubled, divide into 3 equal parts. Place on baking sheet and cover. Let rise again, 15 to 20 minutes in warm place.

7. Roll or stretch each dough piece into a rectangle as thin as you can make it without tearing dough. Brush each rectangle with 2 tablespoons milk, and sprinkle with 1 cup of cinnamon mixture. Roll up snugly like a jelly roll, starting on long edge. Lay dough into "S" shape in a greased, 9- by 5- by 3-inch loaf pan. Let rise until double, about 1 hour.

8. Just before baking, beat remaining egg; brush each loaf with egg. Bake at 350 degrees 35 minutes, or until well browned and slightly crusty on top. Remove from pan at once. Place on rack to cool.

Variations: Dough, without filling, makes good dinner rolls. You also can make a tea ring by adding 1 cup chopped nuts and 1 cup raisins to the cinnamon mixture on each rolled-out rectangle. Form into roll as before, then shape each roll into a ring. Place formed dough on baking sheet. Let rise until double, about 1 hour. To make more attractive, slash top of ring with sharp knife. Bake as before. Frost with confectioners' sugar icing or garnish with maraschino cherries, if desired.

Makes 3 loaves

Whole-Wheat Pita

Peggy Tucker, Pleasant Hill, Missouri

1 tablespoon honey
1 envelope quick-rising yeast
2 cups warm water (110 degrees to
    115 degrees)
1 teaspoon salt
About 5 cups whole-wheat bread
    flour, divided

Peggy used to run a whole-grains bakery: "I found that the people liked the things that I made with the whole-grain flours. It was new to many of the people who came to my shop, and they would be surprised that it could be that good."

1. Dissolve honey and quick-rising yeast in warm water in large bowl. When foamy, add salt and 3 cups flour. Stir and beat well to develop gluten.

2. Continue adding flour in small amounts, beating until dough is too stiff to stir with a spoon. Turn out on floured board. Knead vigorously until dough is firm but supple and elastic, at least 10 minutes.

3. Cover and allow to rise until a wet finger leaves a hole when pressed in, about 30 minutes. Turn out onto table; cut into 12 equal pieces. Form each piece into a ball. Cover with a towel; let rest 5 minutes.

4. Preheat oven to 450 degrees. At the same time, heat clay tile or pizza stone on bottom rack of oven. (If unavailable, use baking sheet.)

5. Roll out a dough ball, dusting with flour as needed to avoid sticking, to 5- to 6-inch circle. Turn dough over and place on lightly floured surface; cover with towel. Allow to rest a few minutes, but not until dough has risen. Repeat with 1 or 2 more balls.

6. When ready to bake, lift pita, and turn with top up. Place 2 to 3 pitas on hot tile, stone or baking sheet on bottom rack of oven. Bake 4 to 5 minutes or until puffed up like a balloon. (Window in oven helps you see when pitas are puffed.)

7. Once puffed, remove to cooling rack; steam inside will finish cooking pitas. When cool, stack and cover to prevent drying.

8. While 1 batch is baking, roll out 2 to 3 more pitas. Wait until oven has returned to 450 degrees before baking. Repeat process for remaining balls.

Note: If pitas do not puff, try kneading the dough more or increasing oven temperature. Do not let tops get too dry.

Makes 1 dozen

Pretzel Animals

Beth Driks, Prairie Village, Kansas

Beth and her three children enjoy making these pretzels together.

1. Preheat oven to 425 degrees. Mix yeast, water, sugar and salt. Stir in flour. Knead until smooth.

2. Shape into pretzel, animal or free-form shapes. Place on ungreased baking sheets.

3. Brush with beaten egg. Sprinkle with kosher salt. (No rising necessary.)

4. Bake 15 until 20 minutes, until browned.

1 envelope active dry yeast
1½ cups warm water
1 tbsp sugar
1 tbsp salt
4 cups all-purpose flour
1 egg, beaten
Kosher salt for sprinkling

Makes about 1 dozen, depending on size of pretzels

Chick-Pea Bread

Margaret Lee, Merriam, Kansas

3 large eggs, lightly beaten
1 tsp cider vinegar
3 tbsp olive oil
1⅓ cups water
¼ tsp gluten-free maple extract,
   optional
1 cup chick-pea flour
1 cup brown or white rice flour
1 cup tapioca flour
½ cup cornstarch
4 tsp xanthan gum
3 tbsp brown sugar
1½ tsp salt
1 tbsp egg replacer (a powdered soy
   product), optional
½ cup dry milk
2¼ tsp active dry yeast

Margaret is an avid quilter who has a machine-quilting business. For health reasons, Margaret uses only gluten-free products so she is always looking for other types of flour. "I just want to live long enough to make every quilt pattern I have ever seen," she says.

1. Combine eggs, vinegar, oil, water and, if desired, maple extract; pour carefully into baking pan of electric breadmaker.

2. In mixing bowl, combine remaining ingredients; mix well. Add dry ingredients to baking pan. Carefully seat pan in breadmaker.

3. Select normal/white cycle, or cycle that is machine's quicker cycle; start machine.

4. After mixing begins, help any unmixed ingredients into the dough with a rubber spatula. Stay to edges and top of batter so as not to interfere with the paddle.

5. When bake cycle is complete, remove pan from machine. Invert pan and shake gently to remove bread. Cool upright on rack before slicing.

Adapted from a recipe from Red Star Yeast & Products.

Notes: Ingredients available at health food stores. All ingredients except yeast should be at room temperature. Humidity and other factors can affect dough consistency, which should be stiffer than cake batter but not as stiff as cookie dough. Add 1 tablespoon liquid at a time if dough is too dry to make consistency that allows machine to mix by itself. For machines with a "bake only" cycle, select "dough" cycle for mixing, stop, then "bake only'" to finish bread.

Makes 1 medium loaf

About the Author

Janet Majure has written "Come Into My Kitchen" for *The Kansas City Star* since March 1992. She has cowritten "Online Epicure®" with Neil Salkind since 1996. A freelance writer and editor since 1989, Majure's work has appeared in numerous newspapers, magazines and books. Before that she was a reporter and editor for daily newspapers in Kansas City, Denver, Phoenix and Tucson.

Majure's cooking career began in her childhood home, where she quickly mastered brownies, became the resident pastry "chef" and learned the perils of not watching her fingers when using a grater or vegetable peeler. She was chief cook for herself and two roommates in college. Majure's cooking skills have been honed since adulthood, even though her daughter, Susan, would happily subsist on none of her mother's cooking.

Majure was born in 1954 in Topeka, Kansas, to Dave and Betty Majure. She grew up with her three sisters—Susan, Joyce and Lori—in Merriam, Kansas. Majure graduated from Shawnee Mission North High School and holds a bachelor's degree in journalism and a master's in business administration from the University of Kansas in Lawrence. She lives with her family in Lawrence.

Index

Order Form

Please send *Recipes Worth Sharing* to me at:

Name _____

Address _____

City _____

State _____

Zip _____

Phone Number (   ) _____

For Gifts: Please send _____ book(s) to:

Name _____

Address _____

City _____

State _____

Zip _____

Gift Card to read: _____

_____

Quantity ____ at $14.95 each = _____

*Shipping: $3 for first book, $1.50 for each additional book	*Shipping _____
	Subtotal _____

KS addresses add 6.9% sales tax _____

Total enclosed _____

Mail order form and check or money order to:

**Breadbasket Publishing Co., Orders Dept.,
P.O. Box 1161, Lawrence, KS 66044-0161**

Order Form

Please send *Recipes Worth Sharing* to me at:

Name _____

Address _____

City _____

State _____

Zip _____

Phone Number (   ) _____

For Gifts: Please send _____ book(s) to:

Name _____

Address _____

City _____

State _____

Zip _____

Gift Card to read: _____

_____

Quantity ____ at $14.95 each = _____

*Shipping: $3 for first book, $1.50 for each additional book	*Shipping _____
	Subtotal _____

KS addresses add 6.9% sales tax _____

Total enclosed _____

Mail order form and check or money order to:

**Breadbasket Publishing Co., Orders Dept.,
P.O. Box 1161, Lawrence, KS 66044-0161**